A
LIFE-SHAPING
PRAYER

A
LIFE-SHAPING
PRAYER

52 Meditations in the Wesleyan Spirit

PAUL WESLEY CHILCOTE

UPPER
ROOM BOOKS®
NASHVILLE

Cover design: Thelma Whitworth/TMW Designs
Cover image: SuperStock
Interior design: Nancy Terzian/Buckinghorse Design
First printing: 2008

LIBRARY OF CONGRESS CATALOGING-IN-PUBLICATION DATA
Chilcote, Paul Wesley
   A life-shaping prayer : 52 meditations in the Wesleyan spirit / Paul Wesley Chilcote.
      p. cm.
   Includes index.
   ISBN 978-0-8358-9938-3
   1. Methodist Church—Prayers and devotions. 2. Spiritual life—Methodist Church. I. Title.
   BX8349.S68C45 2008
   242—dc22   2007045595
Printed in the United States of America

For Steve and Jeannie Harper,
Methodists who practice prayer well,
for whom
to live is to pray
and to pray is to live.

CONTENTS

INTRODUCTION

Christians today are rediscovering what it means to practice the faith. This should be no surprise to Methodists whatsoever. The movement of spiritual renewal led by the Wesleys and others within the Church of England revolved around practicing works of piety and works of mercy. The leaders of Methodism anchored their followers in a holistic spirituality that resisted the separation of faith and practice. Prayer and life, they believed, belong together, and to divorce the life of devotion from the life of service destroys authentic and vital faith. They sought to rediscover what they called primitive Christianity and described the practice of this vision as faith working by love, leading to holiness of heart and life.

The terms *accountable discipleship* and *active faith* reflect the genius of the Methodist movement. The followers of this way founded their lives upon the grace of God, to be sure, but they saw no contradiction between salvation by grace through faith and the necessity of apprenticing themselves to the risen Master. Methodists have always believed that growth in grace depends upon an intentional journeying through life with Jesus as guide, companion, and friend. Yoked with Christ we learn how to love, how to offer our own lives in sacrifice and praise to God, and how to live into God's reign in this world. We say "practice makes perfect," and while the Methodist vision of life's goal is far from some pathological form of perfection*ism*, the spiritual progeny of the Wesleys do turn all their energy in the direction of perfect love of God and neighbor. Practicing faith liberates this love in the practitioner.

In reading through the journal of an early Methodist woman named Elizabeth Rhodes, I was struck (almost overwhelmed actually) by her reference to a prayer she committed to memory as an aspect of her spiritual discipline. Her Methodist mentors taught her to memorize prayers, as well as to master much of the biblical witness. She records the incident of her childhood in these words: "I committed a long Prayer to memory for the purpose of repeating it to the preacher: it was written by Mr. Cozens, a Wesleyan minister; and as it was a great blessing to me, I shall here subjoin it, hoping it may prove of equal benefit to others." Elizabeth's prayer appears on the facing page.

Jonathan Coussins, one of John Wesley's itinerant ministers and the husband of an extremely influential Cheltenham Methodist preacher, Penelope née Newman, almost certainly composed this prayer. The wife, in this instance, converted the husband. The ethos and content of the prayer may owe as much to her as it does to him. Regardless, the two worked side by side and exemplified the essence of the Methodist way. This prayer reflects many of the central themes, values, and goals of vital Christianity they sought to realize in their own lives. When I first encountered this text, it seemed like a prayerful meditation on John Wesley's brief but important treatise "The Character of a Methodist." In my mind's eye, the portrait of a faithful disciple of Christ, schooled in the Methodist way, began to take shape.

*G*rant me, gracious Lord, a pure intention of heart, and a steadfast regard to your glory in all my actions. Possess my mind continually with your presence, and fill it with your love, that my whole delight may be to repose in the arms of your protection. Be light to my eyes, music to my ears, sweetness to my taste, and full contentment to my heart. Be my sunshine in the day, my food at the table, my repose in the night, my clothing in company, my succor in all necessities.

Lord Jesus, I give you my body, my soul, my substance, my fame, my friends, my liberty and my life. Dispose of me, and all that is mine, as seems best to you, and to the glory of your blessed name. I am not my own, but yours; therefore claim me as your right, keep me as your charge, and love me as your child. Fight for me when I am assailed, heal me when I am wounded, and revive me when I am destroyed.

My Lord and my God, I ask you to give me patience in troubles, humility in comforts, constancy in temptations, and victory over all my ghostly enemies. Grant me sorrow for my sins, thankfulness for my benefits, fear of your judgments, love of your mercies, and mindfulness of your presence for evermore. Make me humble to my superiors and friendly to my equals, ready to please all and loathe to offend any; loving to my friends and charitable to my enemies. Give me modesty in my countenance, gravity in my behavior, deliberation in my speech, holiness in my thoughts, and righteousness in all my actions. Let your mercy cleanse me from my sins, and your grace bring forth in me the fruits of everlasting life.

Lord, let me be obedient without arguing, humble without feigning, patient without grudging, pure without corruption, merry without lightness, sad without mistrust, sober without dullness, true without duplicity, fearing you without desperation, and trusting you without presumption. Let me be joyful for nothing but that which pleases you, and sorrowful for nothing but what displeases you: that labor be my delight which is for you, and let all weary me that is not in you. Give me a waking spirit, and a diligent soul, that I may seek to know your will, and when I know it may I perform it faithfully to the honor and glory of your ever blessed name. Amen.

A HELPFUL RESOURCE FOR TODAY

This prayer shaped the life of Elizabeth Rhodes. I am bold to claim that it can be an avenue through which the Spirit forms you and me in Christ as well. After I initially read this prayer, I determined to apprentice myself to its author and to walk beside other Methodists like Elizabeth, who have practiced this way as well. Then, having immersed myself in this prayer for a while, the idea gradually emerged to reconfigure it into a devotional resource. A way forward presented itself immediately.

In the original transcription in her journal, Elizabeth divided the prayer into four roughly equal parts. As I prayed and meditated on each of these sections, a theme for each respective part took shape in my mind in the form of a question:

> Part I: Who is God to me?
> Part II: What can I give to and ask of God?
> Part III: How does God shape my life?
> Part IV: How do I live as a disciple of Christ?

I have subdivided each of these sections into thirteen discrete phrases drawn from the prayer and modernized for the contemporary reader, representing themes related to these questions. A wide range of hymns by Charles Wesley (familiar and unfamiliar) supplements narrative reflections on each theme and phrase in the prayer.

The prayer of Elizabeth's memory opens with the words, "Grant me, gracious Lord." For those who are familiar with liturgical forms of prayer, these words sound much like the petition of a "collect." In Christian worship, a collect functions both as a liturgical action and as a short, general prayer. It usually follows a hymn of praise after the opening of a service of worship. In more ancient practice, the pastor or priest invited the people to spend a short period of time in silent prayer, then "collected" the silent prayers of the people in a unified petition that set the theme for the day. This collect, usually only one sentence in length, included an address to God, reference to an attribute or saving act of God, the petition and its purpose, and a simple doxological conclusion.

While all Methodists may not be familiar with this form of prayer, the collect retains a central place in the *Book of Worship* and *The United Methodist Hymnal*, primarily by means of inheritance from the Book of Common Prayer of the Church of England. Thomas Cranmer, the principal author of this prayer book and liturgical resource used later by the Wesleys, mastered the art of collect prayers. We recite one of his most famous collects at the beginning of the United Methodist service of Word and Table: "Almighty God, to you all hearts are open, all desires known, and from you no secrets are hid: Cleanse the thoughts of our hearts by the inspiration of your Holy Spirit, that we may perfectly love you, and worthily magnify your holy Name; through Christ our Lord. Amen." Many traditional collects petition God by praying: "Grant us, we beseech thee." Similar to the form of the collect, Elizabeth's prayer begins: "Gracious Lord . . . grant me." With Coussins, she turns a corporate act into a personal supplication. The prayer conveys an intimacy, a special connection with the One to whom she prays.

Each week's readings conclude, therefore, with a collect that follows the hymn. This prayer can set the tone for the day or the week. Once you have a sense of the collect for-mula, I encourage you not to depend upon the set form of prayer on the page but to construct your own collect in response to your practice of praying these prayers, singing these hymns, and reflecting upon these meditations. I have provided a template for the basic pattern of the collect at the close of this book for your use.

I pray that God will become increasingly real to you as you use these materials. God has gifted you richly, desires to shape your life through the power of Jesus' love, and yearns for you to show yourself to be a disciple of Christ. The practice of prayer—practicing life in Christ—requires effort, but all begins and ends in God's grace and loving-kindness. Permit the Spirit of God to breathe new life into you, here at the beginning, as you pray these words of Charles Wesley:

> Enlarge, inflame, and fill my heart
> With boundless charity divine!

HOW TO USE THIS BOOK

Each of the fifty-two readings in this book includes a biblical text, a brief meditation, a Wesley hymn selection, and a prayer for the day. The devotional exercise begins, appropriately, in the Word of God. I have provided an index, Scripture Sources Cited, at the end of the book so that you can see the range of biblical material at a single glance. The hymns, almost all of them texts composed by Charles Wesley, are keyed to the themes and scriptural passages proper to each day. The name of a hymn tune recommended for singing the text, as well as the title of a standard hymn sung to the same meter, accompanies each hymn. These suggestions come from *The United Methodist Hymnal*, but the hymn tunes and meters can be located in the index of the standard hymnals of many traditions. The meters of the hymns and the suggested tunes are also collected in an index at the end of the book.

One of the issues I struggle with is the Wesleys' pervasive use of gender-specific language with reference to humanity in the hymns. This certainly distinguishes their age from our own. I am strongly committed to the use of inclusive language in all my writing and teaching. In the preparation of this volume, therefore, I have modernized the hymn texts, not only with reference to gender-specific language related to humanity but also by updating the more archaic expressions unknown to most readers today. I have retained most of Wesley's elisions that clarify the meter or help the musician who elects to sing the texts. Also, in an effort to make the hymns more user-friendly, I have occasionally taken some poetic license with the texts so that they conform more easily to the meter and flow of contemporary hymn tunes. Whenever I have changed the original, I hope I have not altered the meaning or fine poetic diction of the lyrical genius who created them originally. If the reader/singer prefers the use of non-gender-specific language with reference to God, I invite experimentation with the texts. Charles Wesley was more concerned about a healthy and vital relationship with God than he was troubled by the language we use to pray to God or talk with God. The emphasis on relationship strengthens Wesley's poetry, but even such an amazing wordsmith at that time could not appreciate fully how gendered language shapes our basic understandings. Authentic prayer awakens sensitivity, but the Spirit intercedes when language falters and fails.

You can use this resource in a number of ways. Perhaps the most obvious way is to center each week of the year on one of the readings. I have structured the book with this plan in mind, providing readings to accompany the fifty-two weeks of the year. You may read the selection on Sunday, at the beginning of the week, or read it daily throughout the course of the week. In this way you will immerse yourself in the themes of the prayer throughout the course of a full year.

Another practice would be to use the readings at the beginning and ending of each day. At the back of this book you will find a pattern for both Morning and Evening Prayer.

You may insert these devotional materials into these patterns to enhance the time of prayer and meditation. Observing Morning and Evening Prayer is a time-honored practice and a way to feel connected with other disciples in a common pattern of prayer. If you were to pray selections one and two on the first day, three and four on the second, and so forth, through fifty-two, you would make your way through the entire collection in the course of a month (actually twenty-six days with Sundays left out for other religious practices and corporate worship). Seasons such as Advent and Lent would be particularly appropriate times for this approach.

You may wish to read the book straight through. That approach provides the big picture—the panoramic vision. Getting a sense of the whole often helps our attempt to grow into it. But since the readings are passages from the Bible, meditations, hymns, and prayers, they do call for a devotional pace of reading. Time for reflection—allowing the words and images to sink into your spirit—is also important. So take time with the readings, even if you read straight through. Meditate upon them. Ponder the deep meaning of the words, images, and themes that relate to the Triune God's gift of love to the world and to you. A day apart on retreat might provide opportunity to read through the material in each part in a leisurely and spiritually uplifting way. A spiritual retreat of this kind each quarter, perhaps over the course of a weekend, using the four separate parts of the book, might prove to be an extremely beneficial practice.

Yet another option is to read these selections in the order of the biblical books, beginning with passages from the Hebrew scriptures and working your way forward through the Gospels and New Testament writings, rather than follow the order of Elizabeth's prayer. The scripture index at the back of the book provides a road map for this approach if you choose it. Reading this way will create a unique perspective by juxtaposing themes and images in a different way. Note the amazing range and diversity of the biblical material. There is great breadth and depth here.

Finally, these selections might be put to use in corporate contexts, for example, in prayer groups, covenant discipleship groups, Bible studies, class meetings, and Sunday or midweek worship. This approach affords several benefits. Disciplines or practices of the faith often require support. Camaraderie carries us through the more difficult moments. Companionship helps to sustain the journey. Praying and meditating with others also creates the opportunity to learn from one another, to share insights and feelings, and to grow as a community of faith. Perhaps you have a prayer partner with whom you would like to share this experience. I actually envision entire congregations using this book to enrich their spiritual life and incorporate important devotional practices into the rhythm of their common life. Consider the abundance of spiritual fruit produced from a congregation-wide study of these materials. The pattern of Morning and Evening Prayer recommended here is particularly well suited for all of these uses. I particularly encourage pastors to use this book as a resource for public worship.

Open yourself to the leading of the Holy Spirit. However you choose to use this book, approach the experience prayerfully and expectantly. Ask God to speak to you through the means of this early Methodist prayer and the witness of spiritual mentors from the past whose practice continues to encourages us. A great cloud of witnesses surrounds you and cheers you on. Enter into this experience of "practicing a Methodist prayer" as a grace-filled labor of love. May the time you spend in prayer and meditation— practicing your faith—lead naturally into a richer life of enacted love. May you sing with Charles Wesley:

Father, Son, and Spirit, hear
    Faith's effectual, fervent prayer,
Hear and our petitions seal;
    Let us now the answer feel.

Mystically one with thee,
    Transcript of the Trinity,
Thee let all our nature own
    One in three, and three in one.

PART I

Who is God to me?

Grant me, gracious Lord,
a pure intention of heart,
and a steadfast regard to your glory in all my actions.
Possess my mind continually with your presence,
and fill it with your love,
that my whole delight may be to repose
in the arms of your protection.
Be light to my eyes,
music to my ears,
sweetness to my taste,
and full contentment to my heart.
Be my sunshine in the day,
my food at the table,
my repose in the night,
my clothing in company, my succor in all necessities.

WEEK 1

Grant me, gracious Lord

SCRIPTURE

The LORD is gracious and merciful, slow to anger and abounding in steadfast love. The LORD is good to all, and his compassion is over all that he has made. All your works shall give thanks to you, O LORD, and all your faithful shall bless you. They shall speak of the glory of your kingdom, and tell of your power, to make known to all people your mighty deeds, and the glorious splendor of your kingdom. Your kingdom is an everlasting kingdom, and your dominion endures throughout all generations. The LORD is faithful in all his words, and gracious in all his deeds.—Psalm 145:8-13

MEDITATION

Our prayer begins where all prayer must begin, in the realization that the One to whom we speak is a God of grace. We do not say, "Grant me," in the sense of a demand. Rather, we know that the God we worship, like a faithful parent, longs to give us the very best, to offer to us the most wonderful gifts, to fill the deepest desires and longings of our hearts.

To pray to such a God is like falling into the arms of the one you love. You open up your life to the One who is always faithful and trustworthy. You look to God, in the midst of hopelessness and in confidence, during times of deep personal agony and of glorious triumph, from positions of overwhelming abundance and of utter desperation, and you find the Lord already near. In fact, God forms the very center of your life, just waiting to be with you through it all. God's grace will always amaze you. It causes you to be a creature of thankfulness and prayer.

Whenever I hear the word *grant*, I immediately think of the ancient collects of the church. These prayers often include the petition, like this one, "Grant me. . . ." When all is said and done, the deepest prayer of each person's heart is the profound request, "Grant me, Gracious Lord, a living relationship with you, for I know that if I entrust my life to you, I will always be safe."

HYMN

This hymn can be sung to Winchester Old, the tune used for "While Shepherds Watched Their Flocks." Meter CM

Hail, Father, Son, and Holy Ghost,
  One God in Persons Three;
Of thee we make our joyful boast,
  Our songs we make of thee.

Thou lov'st whate'er thy hands have made;
  Thy goodness we rehearse,
In shining characters displayed
  Throughout our universe.

Wherefore let every creature give
>To thee the praise designed;
But chiefly, Lord, the thanks receive,
>The hearts of humankind.

PRAYER

Gracious Lord, you are the beginning and ending of all things, my center and my circumference: root and fix me in you in such a way that my soul finds rest in its true home and never stops growing in grace, safe and secure in your loving embrace. Amen.

WEEK 2

A pure intention of heart

SCRIPTURE

The eye is the lamp of the body. So, if your eye is healthy, your whole body will be full of light; but if your eye is unhealthy, your whole body will be full of darkness. If then the light in you is darkness, how great is the darkness!— Matthew 6:22-23

MEDITATION

Purity of intention characterizes the essence of the Christian life. This means that our one, our singular desire is to please God in all thoughts, words, and actions. Thomas à Kempis, in his great masterpiece of Christian devotion, *The Imitation of Christ*, gives us a marvelous image: simplicity and purity as the two wings that lift the soul up to heaven. Simplicity relates to our intention. Purity describes our affections (II, iv. 1-3). Purity of heart and clarity of intention define life as God has intended it to be lived.

God's grace and activity in our lives move us to the goal of love if we do not resist their influence. Without purity of intention, all our endeavors, all our efforts will be vain and ineffectual. In his Sermon on the Mount, Jesus provides another metaphor to illustrate this essential characteristic of real life. He says that "the eye is the lamp of the body." The eye is to the body what the intention is to the soul. If we fix our eyes upon God—focus upon Jesus—then life will be filled with true happiness and light. Remember, however, that we cannot manufacture this singularity on our own. God's grace must accompany all our efforts to please God and to fulfill God's will in all things great and small. But that which God requires, God provides; all is then light, and our souls are lifted up to the heaven of love.

HYMN

This hymn can be sung to Diademata, the tune used for "Crown Him with Many Crowns." Meter: SMD

God of almighty love,
> By whose sufficient grace
I lift my heart to things above,
> And humbly seek thy face;
> Through Jesus Christ the just
> My faint desires receive,
And let me in thy goodness trust,
> And to thy glory live.

Whate'er I say or do,
> Thy glory be my aim;
My offerings all be offered through
> The ever-blessed Name!
> Jesu, my single eye
> Be fixed on thee alone;
Thy name be praised on earth, on high,
> Thy will by all be done!

PRAYER

Gracious Lord, by whose sufficient grace I lift up my heart in prayer: keep my eye focused upon you at all times, that through purity of intention I might bring honor and praise to your wonderful, glorious, and ever blessed name. Amen.

WEEK 3

And a steadfast regard to your glory in all my actions

SCRIPTURE

Above all, maintain constant love for one another, for love covers a multitude of sins. Be hospitable to one another without complaining. Like good stewards of the manifold grace of God, serve one another with whatever gift each of you has received. Whoever speaks must do so as one speaking the very words of God; whoever serves must do so with the strength that God supplies, so that God may be glorified in all things through Jesus Christ. To him belong the glory and the power forever and ever. Amen.—1 Peter 4:8-11

MEDITATION

It became common in the twentieth century to describe worship as the glorification of God and the sanctification of humanity. Irenaeus, a sainted theologian of the early church, put it all rather simply when he observed that God's greatest glory is the human person fully alive. In prayer, we often begin naturally with a sense of God's glory. When we contemplate the One to whom our prayers ascend, realizing

Who this is can be quite overwhelming. How can I even address a God who has flung one hundred thousand million galaxies into existence out of nothing?

But like Irenaeus, the pray-er of this early Methodist prayer turns the question around to you and to me. *What is it that I can do to bring glory to this God?* There is no sense of arrogance in this bold reversal. Instead, confronted with the reality of this awesome God, the attentive soul responds with deep desire to glorify God through every action, word, and thought—to sanctify life in the glorification of God and to glorify God through the sanctification of life.

Our lives glorify God when we live in loving relationship with one another. Our lives glorify God when we offer hospitality to those who need our care and support. Our lives glorify God when we use the unique gifts that God has given to each of us, not to bring attention to ourselves but for healing, edifying, encouraging, and serving others.

HYMN

This hymn can be sung to Ave Virgo Virginum, the tune used for "Christian People, Raise Your Song." Meter: 76.76 D

Meet and right it is to sing,
    In every time and place,
Glory to our heavenly King,
    The God of truth and grace.
Join we then with sweet accord,
    All in one thanksgiving join:
Holy, holy, holy, Lord,
    Eternal praise be thine!

Thee the first-born sons of light,
    In choral symphonies,
Praise by day, day without night,
    And never, never cease;
Angels and archangels all
    Praise the mystic Three in One,
Sing, and stop, and gaze, and fall
    O'erwhelmed before thy throne.

Father, God, thy love we praise
    Which gave thy Son to die;
Jesus, full of truth and grace,
    Alike we glorify;
Spirit, Comforter divine,
    Praise by all to thee be given,
Till we in full chorus join,
    And earth is turned to heaven.

PRAYER

Gracious Lord, God of truth and grace and love: grant me to praise you, bless you, and worship you through all I think and say and do; for only you, O Christ, with the Holy Spirit, fully radiate the glory of God the Father throughout all ages. Amen.

WEEK 4

Possess my mind continually with your presence, and fill it with your love

SCRIPTURE

For this reason I bow my knees before the Father, from whom every family in heaven and on earth takes its name. I pray that, according to the riches of his glory, he may grant that you may be strengthened in your inner being with power through his Spirit, and that Christ may dwell in your hearts through faith, as you are being rooted and grounded in love. I pray that you may have the power to comprehend, with all the saints, what is the breadth and length and height and depth, and to know the love of Christ that surpasses knowledge, so that you may be filled with all the fullness of God.—Ephesians 3:14-19

MEDITATION

John and Charles Wesley taught their followers about the importance of God's love. For the disciple of Christ, it is not too much to claim that love defines everything. Love teaches us who we are. Love receives us when, in humility and repentance, we turn back to the God who loves us with an immeasurable love. Love restores and heals our soul. Love provides our direction, shapes our actions, and establishes our goals in life. God has constructed us in such a way that love, in fact, should characterize all our relationships.

Created in God's own image—with the capacity to love—we seek to love God with our whole being and to love our neighbors as we love ourselves. Faith is the means to this loving end. In other words, built upon a firm foundation of trust in Christ, our lives move toward the goal of love—the fullest possible love of God and the fullest possible love of all people and things in God. What an audacious vision, to be immersed and lost in God's love! The Wesleys described this goal as *perfect love* or *Christian perfection*. Charles Wesley sings about perfect love in a hymn paraphrase of this passage from Ephesians. We all gasp, he claims, to know such a love. The dimensions are so great that the soul must swell to be filled with all the fullness of God. Is this not the one burning desire of our heart—to be filled, immersed, lost in this love?

HYMN

This hymn can be sung to Toplady, the tune used for "Rock of Ages, Cleft for Me." Meter: 66.77.77

> To love is all my wish,
> I only live for this:
> Grant me, Lord, my heart's desire,
> There by faith for ever dwell.
> This I always will require,
> Thee, and only thee to feel.

Thy power I pant to prove,
Rooted and fixed in love;
Strengthened by thy Spirit's might,
Wise to fathom things divine,
What the length, and breadth, and height,
What the depth of love like thine.

Ah! give me this to know,
With all thy saints below;
Swells my soul to compass thee;
Gasps in thee to live and move;
Filled with all the Deity,
All immersed and lost in love!

PRAYER

Gracious Lord, you fully know and fully love all you have created: grant me power to comprehend the breadth and length and height and depth, and to know the love of Christ that surpasses knowledge, that I might be immersed and lost in your love. Amen.

WEEK 5

That my whole delight may be to repose in the arms of your protection

SCRIPTURE

There is none like unto the God of Jeshurun, who rideth upon the heaven in thy help, and in his excellency on the sky. The eternal God is thy refuge, and underneath are the everlasting arms: and he shall thrust out the enemy from before thee; and shall say, Destroy them. Israel then shall dwell in safety alone: the fountain of Jacob shall be upon a land of corn and wine; also his heavens shall drop down dew. Happy art thou, O Israel: who is like unto thee, O people saved by the LORD, the shield of thy help.—Deuteronomy 33:26-29, KJV

MEDITATION

The historic liturgy for Evening Prayer, prayed daily by the Wesleys, opens with the following cry to the Lord: "O God, make speed to save us. O Lord, make haste to help us." In many of the Psalms, the petition is more personal. "Be pleased, O Lord, to deliver *me*. . . . make haste to help *me*." Supplications such as these, in fact, pervade the Psalter.

Their character is primal, urgent, existential. The simple prayer "deliver me," or "save me," appears no less than twenty-five times in the songs of David alone. As if making his appeal in response to the common experience of all who seek God, the psalmist prays for deliverance from enemies, persecutors, and evildoers; for rescue from violence, strife, and affliction; but also for salvation from guilt and shame as the consequences of personal sin.

People of faith know where to turn for safety; they find repose in the arms of God's protection. The mystery of suffering and affliction may not resolve into simple explanations and ease in life, but in the promise of God's loving care, we feel secure. Martin Luther captured the essence of this dependency in his most famous hymn, "Ein' feste Burg ist unser Gott," a paraphrase of Psalm 46. God, he sings, is a safe stronghold still—a mighty fortress. No matter how the words are translated into English—a bulwark never failing, a sword and shield victorious, a trusty shield and weapon—God is our refuge. Underneath all that perplexes us in life are God's everlasting arms.

HYMN

This hymn can be sung to Canonbury, the tune used for "Lord, Speak to Me." Meter: LM

> How do thy mercies close me round!
>> For ever be thy name adored!
> I blush in all things to abound;
>> The servant is above his Lord!
>
> But lo! a place he hath prepared
>> For me, whom watchful angels keep;

Yea, he himself becomes my guard;
>He smooths my bed, and gives me sleep.

Jesus protects; my fears be gone!
>What can the Rock of Ages move?
Safe in thy arms I lay me down,
>Thy everlasting arms of love.

PRAYER

Gracious Lord, mighty fortress in whom I can always trust: deliver me from whatever shakes my world, fills me with anxiety, and separates me from the knowledge of your love, that I might find repose in your arms of protection. Amen.

WEEK 6

Be light to my eyes

SCRIPTURE

This is the message we have heard from him and proclaim to you, that God is light and in him there is no darkness at all. . . . if we walk in the light as he himself is in the light, we have fellowship with one another, and the blood of Jesus his Son cleanses us from all sin.—1 John 1:5, 7

MEDITATION

It is virtually impossible to conceive of *nothing*. Perhaps I had something of a philosophical bent as a child, because I remember pondering the question of nothing. My father once had preached a sermon on creation, in which he said God created everything that exists out of nothing. As hard as I tried, I could never seem to find my way back to nothing. One thing was clear to me, however. Whatever nothing was, it was dark. Light seemed to have a lot to do with God and the created world in which we live. "Let there be light" explained a lot to me in the midst of my quandary.

Early Jewish Christians who attempted to translate the Christian message into a vocabulary and into thought forms that made sense to the Greeks frequently employed the contrasting images of light and darkness. Our text for today from First John stands within this tradition. God is light. Light dispels the darkness. To be a follower of Christ means that we walk in the light. Charles Wesley's hymn on creation develops the same themes and links the image of light, in particular, to God's re-creative activity in our lives. In the same way that God penetrated darkness with glorious, creative light at the beginning of time, God sends the Son—the light of the world—into the darkness of our hearts. The indwelling Christ empowers us, as God's children, to declare the wonderful deeds of the One who calls us out of darkness into this marvelous light.

HYMN

This hymn can be sung to Carey's (Surrey), the tune used for "Give Me the Faith Which Can Remove." Meter: 88.88.88

Expand thy wings, celestial Dove,
    And brooding o'er my nature's night
Call forth the ray of heavenly love,
    Let there in my dark soul be light;
And fill th'illustrated abyss
With glorious beams of endless bliss.

Let there be light (again command),
    And light there in our hearts shall be;
We then through faith shall understand
    Thy great mysterious majesty,
And by the shining of thy grace
Behold in Christ thy glorious face.

PRAYER

Gracious Lord, God of Light and Love, you long for us to walk, not like children of the darkness nor the night, but like children of the light and of the day: Grant me a steady journey on the highway of holiness toward the light of the city of God, even Christ my Lord. Amen.

WEEK 7

Music to my ears

SCRIPTURE

Above all, clothe yourselves with love, which binds everything together in perfect harmony. And let the peace of Christ rule in your hearts, to which indeed you were called in the one body. And be thankful. Let the word of Christ dwell in you richly; teach and admonish one another in all wisdom; and with gratitude in your hearts sing psalms, hymns, and spiritual songs to God. And whatever you do, in word or deed, do everything in the name of the Lord Jesus, giving thanks to God the Father through him.—Colossians 3:14-17

MEDITATION

Charles Wesley loved music. With two sons who were musical prodigies, Charles and Sally Wesley's home was always filled with the sounds of instruments and voices raised in song. Little wonder that Charles turned to the metaphors of music and song to describe the life of the community of faith—the people of God bound together by the love of Christ. For the believer, life is a concert of praise; indeed, one's whole life is a song to be sung, a melodious act of gratitude to the One who has given us life and redeemed us by grace. But while solos have their place, it is a chorus—the whole company of God's faithful people—that sings "Holy, holy, holy Lord, God of power and might. Heaven and earth are full of your glory." Wesley, in his hymn, describes a "rapturous song" of a "glorified throng" whose sacrifice of praise is the perfect harmony of lives tuned to the keynote of Christ's love. The Hebrew word *hallelujah*—[let us] praise God—captures the spirit of the choir and the nature of the song. According to Paul, more than anything else, thanksgiving and gratitude characterize life in Christ. If we surround ourselves with the love of Jesus—if the love of God envelops us in the same way that our clothes cover our bodies—then God gifts the community and the world with harmony. Peace rules. Unity prevails. All creation becomes a song of praise. What part do you play in this great harmony of the ages?

HYMN

This hymn can be sung to "Trust and Obey," without the added refrain. Meter: 669 D

> Who on earth can conceive
> > Just how happy we live
> In the palace of God, the great King?
> > What a concert of praise,
> > When our Jesus's grace
> The whole heavenly company sing!
>
> > What a rapturous song
> > When the glorified throng
> In the spirit of harmony join!

Join we all the glad choirs,
All our voices and lyres,
And the burden is mercy divine.

Hallelujah they cry
To the King of the sky,
To the great everlasting I AM,
To the Lamb that was slain
Who now liveth again—
Hallelujah to God and the Lamb.

PRAYER

Gracious Lord, you sang all that exists into being: give me a voice to sing your praise in all that I do, a heart to seek harmony with all your creation, and a spirit of gratitude and thanksgiving to tune my heart to the keynote of my life, my Lord, Jesus Christ. Amen.

WEEK 8

Sweetness to my taste

SCRIPTURE

Oh, how I love your law!
It is my meditation all day long.
Your commandment makes me wiser than my enemies,
for it is always with me.
I have more understanding than all my teachers,
for your decrees are my meditation.
I understand more than the aged,
for I keep your precepts.
I hold back my feet from every evil way,
in order to keep your word.
I do not turn away from your ordinances,
for you have taught me.
How sweet are your words to my taste,
sweeter than honey to my mouth!—Psalm 119:97-103

MEDITATION

The poet theologian George Herbert exerted a tremendous
influence upon Charles Wesley. His collection of poems entitled *The Temple* reveals his own personal quest for faith in

and intimacy with God. In a poem built around the image of banquet, Herbert invites Christ to live and dwell in his heart and welcomes the delicious, sacred cheer that surpasses all other earthy joys. Using images common to the mystical tradition, he reflects upon the way in which God's sweetness surprises and deluges the soul. The psalmist describes God's speech—God's Law—in similar ways. God's words are "sweeter than honey to my mouth." What a phenomenal description of God and God's actions!

Recent studies demonstrate that most people conceive God as adversarial, critical, and distant. In terms of taste, it would probably be right to describe their concept—their taste—of God as bitter, sour, and acrid. But those who have come to know God in Jesus Christ have a very different conception. God's Word is sweet. God's law, God's commandments, God's words not only seem sweet but create sweetness. They sweeten everything they touch. In this unique way of thinking about our relationship with God, God delights in providing a banquet of sweet things for us. God invites all who are hungry and thirsty—all who seek mercy and salvation—to come, to drink, and to eat. God offers us the most nourishing food imaginable and shares the sweetness of Christ's mercy with us all.

O God, be sweetness to my taste.

HYMN

This hymn can be sung to Cornish, the tune used for "Your Love, O God, Has Called Us Here." Meter: LM

> Ho! everyone that thirsts, draw nigh,
>> ('Tis God invites the fallen race),

Mercy and free salvation buy;
    Buy wine, and milk, and gospel grace.

Hearken to me with earnest care,
    And freely eat substantial food;
The sweetness of my mercy share,
    And taste that I alone am good.

I bid you all my goodness prove;
    My promises for all are free;
Come, taste the manna of my love,
    And let your soul delight in me.

PRAYER

Gracious Lord, whose words are sweet and whose law of love delights the soul: when I am hungry and thirsty for that which is truly good, welcome me to your great banquet and feed me from the twin tables of your Word and Sacrament so that I might be filled. Amen.

WEEK 9

And full contentment to my heart

SCRIPTURE

I rejoice in the Lord greatly that now at last you have revived your concern for me; indeed, you were concerned for me, but had no opportunity to show it. Not that I am referring to being in need; for I have learned to be content with whatever I have. I know what it is to have little, and I know what it is to have plenty. In any and all circumstances I have learned the secret of being well-fed and of going hungry, of having plenty and of being in need. I can do all things through him who strengthens me.—Philippians 4:10-13

MEDITATION

True contentment eludes many people. Elizabeth's prayer asks God to be the source and the object of the fullest possible contentment. Certainly we live into such a sense of well-being over time and through the various experiences of life that confirm God's trustworthiness. Like a child, we have to learn to trust. Full contentment seldom comes immediately; we practice our way into it.

Paul wrote his letter to the Philippians from prison. He had endured much for the sake of the Lord. And yet, even in this circumstance, he learned to be content. The early Methodist people practiced the art of godly trust. They discovered profound mentors in Charles and Sally Wesley in this regard. The couple's home, filled with all the agony and ecstasy that is part and parcel of family life, glowed with a certain warmth and security born of trust in God.

One of Charles's hymns written for families reflects the spirit of their life together. In the midst of silent tears and boding fears, Christ proved his love and care, over and over again. Mercy flies to their rescue. Before the face of God, even death loosens its grip. Jesus offers no easy panacea for life's troubles, but, even in the midst of grief, the believer holds fast to Jesus' presence. God's perfect strength never fails; when we are weak, God's word of promise raises us above all fear and hopelessness in life. Full contentment depends upon relationships of trust—miracles of grace.

HYMN

This hymn can be sung to Amsterdam, the tune used for "Praise the Lord Who Reigns Above." Meter: 76.76.77.76

Better than my boding fears
    To me thou oft hast proved,
Oft observed my silent tears,
    And challenged thy beloved;
Mercy to my rescue flew;
Death ungrasped his fainting prey;
Pain before thy face withdrew,
    And sorrow fled away.

Now as yesterday the same,
      In all my troubles nigh,
Jesus, on thy word and name
      I steadfastly rely.
Sure as now the grief I feel;
Promised joy I soon shall have;
      Saved again, to sinners tell
         Thy power and will to save.

To thy blessed will resigned,
      And stayed on that alone,
I thy perfect strength shall find,
      Thy faithful mercies own;
Compassed round with songs of praise,
All to Jesus now I give,
      Spread thy miracles of grace,
         And to thy glory live.

PRAYER

Gracious Lord, strength of the weak and ever-present help in time of need: grant me the grace to trust you in all things and to find you present in every circumstance, for my heart will never find perfect peace or full contentment until it rests in you. Amen.

WEEK 10

Be my sunshine in the day

SCRIPTURE

In the beginning was the Word, and the Word was with God, and the Word was God. He was in the beginning with God. All things came into being through him, and without him not one thing came into being. What has come into being in him was life, and the life was the light of all people. The light shines in the darkness, and the darkness did not overcome it. . . . The true light, which enlightens everyone, was coming into the world.—John 1:1-5, 9

MEDITATION

Light, as we have already seen, figures prominently in Elizabeth's prayer and surfaces several times. Charles Wesley filled his sacred poetry with allusions to the light. Some of his most powerful hymns celebrate the light of Christ. Few compare to his "Morning Hymn," however, more generally known by its first line, "Christ, whose glory fills the skies." The contrasting images of the second stanza emphasize the importance of the light of Christ in our lives. Journeying through our days without Christ as our companion results in a dark and joyless life. But when the beams of God's mercy break through the clouds of this gloomy world, the illumination of the Son warms our hearts and cheers our eyes. The darkness cannot overcome this light, for Jesus is the true and only *Light*, the *Sun of Righteousness*, the *Dayspring*, the *Daystar* who arises in our hearts with healing in his wings. The light of Christ penetrates to the depth of our very being, pierces our gloom, scatters our unbelief, and shines through our lives into the world.

The writer of John's Gospel connects this light with life. Apart from this light, life is but a shadow land. The good news is that God shines this light into the life of every person. The Wesleys celebrated this prevenient grace—this offer of God's love extended to everyone before any even know the difference between the darkness and the light. John and Charles Wesley devoted their ministry to showing people how to open the window of their soul to let in the light.

HYMN

This hymn can be sung to Ratisbon, its traditional setting. Meter: 77.77.77

> Christ, whose glory fills the skies,
>> Christ, the true, the only light,
> Sun of Righteousness, arise,
>> Triumph o'er the shades of night;
> Dayspring from on high, be near;
>> Daystar, in my heart appear.

> Dark and cheerless is the morn
>> Unaccompanied by thee;
> Joyless is the day's return,

Till thy mercy's beams I see;
Till they inward light impart,
    Cheer my eyes and warm my heart.

Visit then this soul of mine;
    Pierce the gloom of sin and grief;
Fill me, Radiancy divine,
    Scatter all my unbelief;
More and more thyself display,
    Shining to the perfect day.

PRAYER

Gracious Lord, God from God, light from light, true God from true God, you enlighten every person coming into this world: visit my soul today, pierce the darkness that surrounds me, and fill me with your radiant presence that others might encounter your light in me. Amen.

WEEK 11

My food at the table

SCRIPTURE

The LORD upholds all who are falling,
> and raises up all who are bowed down.

The eyes of all look to you,
> and you give them their food in due season.

You open your hand,
> satisfying the desire of every living thing.

The LORD is just in all his ways,
> and kind in all his doings.

The LORD is near to all who call on him,
> to all who call on him in truth.

He fulfills the desire of all who fear him;
> he also hears their cry, and saves them.

—Psalm 145:14-19

MEDITATION

When I was in high school, our church choir sang an amazing anthem based on Psalm 145:15-16. Every now and then the haunting melody of "The Eyes of All Wait Upon Thee" floats into my consciousness, bringing with it a flood of memories and a sense of God's presence and provision. The psalmist envisions a world in which God provides for our needs—both physical and spiritual—and God's plentiful gifts satisfy everyone. The human family struggles to realize that vision in a broken world, despite the fact that we are united in our need. Perhaps this is one reason why Jean Berger composed his anthem with all voices singing the same rhythm at the same time—one united chorus.

Like the anthem, the needs of the world often build to a climax until we realize that only God can satisfy the desire of every living thing. In the midst of our need, one fact remains clear: God provides enough to satisfy every person on this globe in every possible way. Whenever we gather around the Lord's Table to celebrate our Family Meal, God reminds us through this sign-act of love that Christ satisfies all our needs. But the Table also stands as a reminder to us of those who have no food. The Bread of Life offers himself for us, satisfies the desire of every heart, and invites us to become his body—God's provision—in the world. That is part of what it means to grow up to Christ in all things (Eph. 4:15).

HYMN

This hymn can be sung to Unser Herrscher, the tune used for "God of Love and God of Power." Meter: 77.77.77

> Of all life thou art the tree
> My own immortality!
> Feed this tender branch of thine,
> Ceaseless influence derive;
> Thou the true, the heavenly vine,
> Grafted into thee I live.

Thou art now my daily bread;
O Lord Christ, thou art my head!
Motion, virtue, strength to me,
Me, thy living member, flow;
Nourished I, and fed by thee,
Up to thee in all things grow.

PRAYER

Gracious Lord, you are the Bread of Life, who provides for all my needs and satisfies the deepest longing of my heart: graft me into the very center of your great tree of life; feed me, nourish me, and care for me like a tender vine that I might grow into Christ in all things. Amen.

WEEK 12

My repose in the night

SCRIPTURE

Come to me, all you that are weary and are carrying heavy burdens, and I will give you rest. Take my yoke upon you, and learn from me; for I am gentle and humble in heart, and you will find rest for your souls. For my yoke is easy, and my burden is light.—Matthew 11:28-30

MEDITATION

I suspect that many readers immediately recognize the scripture reading from Matthew's Gospel and have found it meaningful over the years. Who has never felt worn out by life? Who has never sought rest from toil? Jesus promises rest to those who link their lives with his own. He offers us a yoke, a harness that enables him to share our life and our work. He comes alongside to lead, to guide, and to support. He says, in essence, that we need never be alone. Jesus offers his companionship and accompanies us into every labor, every circumstance in life. Not only that: we learn from him as we live and work side by side. His own gentleness and humility rub off on us as we practice faith with the master, as we apprentice our very life to the One who is life itself. And at the end of our day and the end of our days, we find repose in him.

John Wesley translated a German hymn by Gerhard Tersteegen that reflects upon the human yearning for repose—rest in the knowledge that all things will be well—in our lives. He uses the word *repose* twice in his translation. In the first instance, it signifies the deep longing in our hearts; we sigh for this rest. But it is also the realization that when Christ rules the heart, when no rival usurps the unfathomed love God offers to us in him, this gift of repose liberates us to be God's true children.

HYMN

This hymn can be sung to Vater Unser, its traditional setting. Meter: 88.88.88

> Thou hidden love of God, whose height,
>> Whose depth unfathomed, no one knows;
> I see from far thy beauteous light,
>> Inward I sigh for thy repose;
> My heart is pained, nor can it be
> At rest, till it finds rest in thee.

> Is there a thing beneath the sun
>> That strives with thee my heart to share?
> Ah! tear it thence, and reign alone,
>> The Lord of every motion there!
> Then shall my heart from earth be free,
> When it hath found repose in thee.

PRAYER

Gracious Lord, rest of the weary and gentle guardian of the way: come along side me and ease my burden, for I offer myself to you as the apprentice of your gentle and humble way that I might find repose in you in the course of my days and throughout all eternity. Amen.

WEEK 13

My clothing in company, my succor in all necessities

SCRIPTURE

Therefore I tell you, do not worry about your life, what you will eat or what you will drink, or about your body, what you will wear. Is not life more than food, and the body more than clothing? Look at the birds of the air; they neither sow nor reap nor gather into barns, and yet your heavenly Father feeds them. Are you not of more value than they? And can any of you by worrying add a single hour to your span of life? And why do you worry about clothing? Consider the lilies of the field, how they grow; they neither toil nor spin, yet I tell you, even Solomon in all his glory was not clothed like one of these. But if God so clothes the grass of the field, which is alive today and tomorrow is thrown into the oven, will he not much more clothe you—you of little faith? Therefore do not worry, saying, "What will we eat?" or "What will we drink?" or "What will we wear?" For it is the Gentiles who strive for all these things; and indeed your heavenly Father knows that you need all these things. But strive first for the kingdom of God and his righteousness, and all these things will be given to you as well.—Matthew 6:25-33

MEDITATION

Jonathan Coussins, the author of Elizabeth's prayer, con-
cludes the opening section with a return to the theme of
God's provision. God blesses us with light, music, sweetness, and contentment; gives us sunshine, food, and repose;
and provides all the basic necessities of life. Neither
Elizabeth, however, nor the preacher of the Sermon on the
Mount (Matt. 6) viewed God as a heavenly vendor of material and spiritual blessings. That is not the point.

One of the words in Elizabeth's prayer provides a clue,
perhaps, to the important teaching of Jesus and the intent
of this prayer. The somewhat archaic term *succor* comes
from two Latin words, a preposition that means "beneath"
or "under" and a verb that means "to run." So the word literally means "to run beneath" or "to quickly get under." No
less than five times in the portion of his sermon, Jesus
draws attention to the anxious thoughts of the poor who
gathered around him for a word of hope. In the face of their
anxiety, he affirms repeatedly that God will run beneath
them. God will get under them quickly and never let them
fall. Jesus calls them to the joyous abandon of trust in this
God. He himself lived in that sort of relationship with God.
When we cast our care on God (see 1 Pet. 5:7)—when we
live in the joyous abandon of a trusting relationship with
God—glory brings to completion that which grace has
begun in our lives.

HYMN

This hymn can be sung to Candler, the tune used for "Come, O Thou Traveler Unknown." Meter: LMD

Son of thy Sire's eternal love,
  Take to thyself thy mighty power;
Let every child thy mercy prove,
  Let all thy bleeding grace adore.
The triumphs of thy love display,
  In every heart reign thou alone,
Till all thy foes confess thy sway,
  And glory ends what grace begun.

Father, 'tis thine each day to yield
  Thy children's wants a fresh supply;
Thou clothest the lilies of the field,
  And hearest the young ravens cry.
On thee we cast our care; we live
  Through thee, who knowest our every need;
O feed us with thy grace, and give
  Our souls this day the living bread.

PRAYER

Gracious Lord, you provide succor in all necessities in life and sustain your creation each day: quickly get under me when I begin to falter, run beneath me when I am falling, free me from all my anxious thoughts and into the joyful abandon of trust in you. Amen.

PART II

What can I give to and ask of God?

Lord Jesus, I give you my body,
my soul,
my substance, my fame, my friends,
my liberty and my life.
Dispose of me, and all that is mine, as seems best to you,
and to the glory of your blessed name.
I am not my own, but yours;
therefore claim me as your right,
keep me as your charge,
and love me as your child.
Fight for me when I am assailed,
heal me when I am wounded,
and revive me when I am destroyed.

WEEK 14

Lord Jesus, I give you my body

SCRIPTURE

Do you not know that your body is a temple of the Holy Spirit within you, which you have from God, and that you are not your own? For you were bought with a price; therefore glorify God in your body.—1 Corinthians 6:19-20

MEDITATION

God created human beings as a miraculous synergy of body and soul. Belief in the unity of soul and body distinguished early Christians and Jews from their counterparts in Roman culture. Unlike dualists at that time (as well as today) who divorced material and spiritual things, they valued both. No act demonstrated the value God places on our bodies and material existence more than the Incarnation. The word literally means "in-fleshed." God "got" physical in Christ Jesus. God embraces creation in the most radical way imaginable. A handmaiden's son "em-bodies" God. And in his earthly ministry, Jesus spends much of his time healing, feeding, even resurrecting bodies from death. He offers his body for the life of the world and Paul refers to the new community birthed by the Spirit as the body of Christ.

In a culture obsessed with the body, we do well to remember that the body is not something to be worshiped, but neither is it something to be denigrated. Our identity as the children of God derives from our good bodies as much as it does from our good souls. The body, as Paul taught the Corinthians, is a temple of the Holy Spirit—a sacred place in which God dwells. Charles Wesley frequently observed that we worship God with both our physical and our spiritual being. We glorify God in our body as well as our spirit since both belong to God.

HYMN

This hymn can be sung to Aberystwyth, the tune used for "Jesus, Lover of My Soul." Meter: 77.77 D

Holy Ghost, we know thou art
Still in every faithful heart;
Yes; we tremble, Lord, to know
God resides in each below!
O might all our bodies be
Sensibly replete with thee,
O might all thy temples shine
Bright with holiness Divine!

PRAYER

Gracious Lord, who created us as a unity of body and soul: keep me outwardly in my body and inwardly in my soul, that I may be defended from all adversities which may happen to the body and from all evil which may assault and hurt the soul; through Jesus Christ. Amen.

WEEK 15

My soul

SCRIPTURE

His heart is ashes, his hope is cheaper than dirt, and his life is of less worth than clay, because he failed to know the one who formed him and inspired him with an active soul and breathed into him a living spirit.—Wisdom of Solomon 15:10-11, RSV

MEDITATION

Given the fact that body and soul interconnect so inextricably for the Christian, not only do we offer our body to God, but we pray to give God our soul as well. The scripture reading for today uses very interesting language to describe the soul as an essential part of who we are as God's creatures. While unfamiliar to most Protestants, Roman Catholic and Eastern Orthodox Christians find Wisdom of Solomon in a section of the Bible known as the Apocrypha ("secondary" or "hidden" works). As dutiful priests of the Church of England, both John and Charles Wesley read regularly from these apocryphal writings, since they were highly valued in their Anglican tradition.

The author of Wisdom elevates the importance of acknowledging the One who has "inspired" us with "active souls" and a "living spirit." God inspires human beings, literally meaning that God puts a spirit within us ("in-spirits" us). Note the close connection between *incarnation* and *inspiration* used in this sense. The former connected God's Spirit with a body—Jesus' body—in space and time. The latter connects our bodies with an eternal soul. God intends for the soul to act and live, not to atrophy and die. According to Wesley in the hymn below, God creates us to be just and good, full of power and love. But God must restore the misdirected soul to its primitive or original design. God's re-creative work in Christ restores truth, mercy, wisdom, purity, happiness, and most importantly, eternal rest in God's embrace.

HYMN

This hymn can be sung to Amsterdam, the tune used for "Praise the Lord Who Reigns Above." Meter: 76.76.77.76

> Maker, Lord of humankind,
>> Who hast on me bestowed
> An immortal soul, designed
>> To be the house of God,
> Come, and now reside in me,
>> Never, never to remove;
> Make me just, and good, like thee,
>> And full of power and love!
>
> Bid me in thy image rise,
>> A saint, a creature new,
> True, and merciful, and wise,
>> And pure and happy too.
> This thy primitive design,

That I should in thee be blest,
Should within the arms divine
For ever, ever rest.

PRAYER

Gracious Lord, who created us as a unity of body and soul: keep me outwardly in my body and inwardly in my soul, that I may be defended from all adversities which may happen to the body and from all evil which may assault and hurt the soul; through Jesus Christ. Amen.

WEEK 16

My substance, my fame, my friends

SCRIPTURE

Yours, O LORD, are the greatness, the power, the glory, the victory, and the majesty; for all that is in the heavens and on the earth is yours; yours is the kingdom, O LORD, and you are exalted as head above all. Riches and honor come from you, and you rule over all. In your hand are power and might; and it is in your hand to make great and to give strength to all. And now, our God, we give thanks to you and praise your glorious name.

But who am I, and what is my people, that we should be able to make this freewill offering? For all things come from you, and of your own have we given you.—1 Chronicles 29:11-14

MEDITATION

As we continue to explore the question of what we can give to God, our readings today startle us with a critical realization. What we give to God has already come from God. This is particularly hard to hear because we like to believe that substance, fame, and friends are blessings we cultivate in our lives. They are the products of our hard labor. But Wesley sings, "Now I give thee back thine own: Freedom, friends, and health, and fame."

The reading from 1 Chronicles opens with a litany celebrating God's greatness, power, glory, victory, and majesty! All things in the heavens and earth belong to God. Given the fact that everything comes from God, our only appropriate response to all of life's blessings is gratitude and thanks.

Gratitude is an attitude. Material blessings, the acclamation of others, and the support of those who genuinely care for us in life, all provide an opportunity to cultivate a spirit either of gratitude or of prideful arrogance. Thanks emanates from an attitude of gratitude. But how do we cultivate this spirit, this attitude, this response? Perhaps here more than anywhere else, the key is practice. We practice giving thanks. We make it a habit, a habituated pattern of life. We permit God's Spirit to shape us eucharistically through our actions. Increasingly, we discover that our heart and mind and life acclaim: "And now, our God, we give thanks to you, and praise your glorious name."

HYMN

This hymn can be sung to Dix, the tune used for "For the Beauty of the Earth." Meter: 77.77.77

> Now, O God, thine own I am,
>   Now I give thee back thine own:
> Freedom, friends, and health, and fame,
>   Consecrate to thee alone;
> Thine I live, thrice happy I!
> Happier still if thine I die.

Father, Son, and Holy Ghost,
    One in Three, and Three in One,
As by the celestial host
    Let thy will on earth be done:
Praise by all to thee be given,
Glorious Lord of earth and heaven!

PRAYER

Gracious Lord, the author and giver of all good things: graft into my heart the love of your name, nourish all goodness in me, and enable me to offer my very best back to you, for the greatness, the power, the glory, the victory, and the majesty are yours, now and forever. Amen.

WEEK 17

My liberty and my life

SCRIPTURE

Let the same mind be in you that was in Christ Jesus,
who, though he was in the form of God,
did not regard equality with God
as something to be exploited,
but emptied himself,
taking the form of a slave,
being born in human likeness.
And being found in human form,
he humbled himself
and became obedient to the point of
death—
even death on a cross.—Philippians 2:5-8

MEDITATION

The early Christian community sang about the way in which Christ Jesus emptied himself and took on the form of a servant. Paul records this hymn in the second chapter of his letter to the Philippians. It is one the most profound statements about God in the New Testament. Both God's action and the form God assumed in Christ must have amazed and bewildered many who heard the claim. First, he emptied himself. In an effort to explain this act of humility, Charles Wesley said that he "emptied himself of all but love." Divested of all things divine, Jesus Christ, the second Person of the Trinity, remained God, because God is love. Second, he took on the form of a servant. The original Greek of Paul's letter means more literally, a slave. Christ Jesus offered his freedom and life to the redemptive purposes of the Godhead. He sacrificed his liberty to fully emancipate all people; in order to provide a means for every person to experience abundant life, he sacrificed his own life.

In the face of God's action for us, is it too great a thing for us to give God our liberty and life? Notice Wesley's pervasive use of the word *all* in his hymn of dedication. Serving God means to give God our all: All my actions, words, and thoughts; all I have; all I am; all my goods and hours; all I know and feel; all I think and speak and do. Wesley sums up this all-embracing consecration of liberty and life to God in the simple prayer, "take my heart," for in our heart lies our all.

HYMN

This hymn can be sung to Dix, the tune used for "For the Beauty of the Earth." Meter: 77.77.77

> If so small a child as I
>> May to thy great glory live,
> All my actions sanctify,
>> All my words and thoughts receive;
> Claim me for thy service claim
> All I have, and all I am.

Take my soul and body's powers;
    Take my memory, mind, and will;
All my goods, and all my hours,
    All I know, and all I feel!
All I think, and speak, and do;
Take my heart: but make it new!

PRAYER

Gracious Lord, you emptied yourself, took on the form of a servant, and became obedient unto death in order to break the tyranny of sin: grant me grace to dedicate my freedom to your service, that all humanity may be brought to the glorious liberty of the children of God. Amen.

WEEK 18

Dispose of me, and all that is mine, as seems best to you

SCRIPTURE

I appeal to you therefore, brothers and sisters, by the mercies of God, to present your bodies as a living sacrifice, holy and acceptable to God, which is your spiritual worship. Do not be conformed to this world, but be transformed by the renewing of your minds, so that you may discern what is the will of God—what is good and acceptable and perfect.—Romans 12:1-2

MEDITATION

The so-called Covenant Prayer remains one the most important and cherished prayers of the Methodist heritage. John Wesley adapted it from the service of covenant renewal developed by an English Puritan named Richard Alleine. Many Methodists throughout the history of the movement have prayed this prayer at the beginning of each new year as they have sought to claim God's covenant anew in their lives.

Perhaps the petition of our prayer for today reminds some readers of several lines from that corporate act of rededication (and others we will explore in later weeks): "I am no longer my own, but thine. Put me to what thou wilt. . . . I freely and heartily yield all things to thy pleasure and disposal." Paul's words to the Roman church reflect this same spirit. He admonishes the followers of Christ to present the fullness of their lives as a living sacrifice to God. True worship, the apostle claims, consists in this oblation. We offer who we are and what we have, all our accomplishments and aspirations, all our hopes and dreams, as a joyful response to the immeasurable love God offers us in Christ. Wesley's hymn recapitulates the constitutive aspects of this living sacrifice, explored these past weeks. We present our souls and bodies to God. All that comes from God we gratefully return with thanks and praise. God declares the gift of our all to be holy and acceptable when we join it to the sacrifice of the all-atoning Lamb.

HYMN

This hymn can be sung to Gift of Love, the tune used for "The Gift of Love." Meter: LM

Father, our sacrifice receive;
souls and bodies we present,
Our goods, and vows, and praises give,
Whate'er thy bounteous love hath lent.

Thou canst not now our gift despise,
Cast on that all-atoning Lamb,
Mixed with that bleeding sacrifice,
And offered up through Jesu's name.

PRAYER

Gracious Lord, God of power and might, you have revealed that true strength lies in self-surrender and sacrifice by the way in which Jesus emptied himself of all but love: shape me into a true disciple through my own self-emptying and sacrifice, for Jesus' sake. Amen.

WEEK 19

And to the glory of your blessed name

SCRIPTURE

They lift up their voices, they sing for joy;
>>they shout from the west over the majesty of the Lord.
Therefore in the east give glory to the Lord;
>>in the coastlands of the sea glorify the name
>>>of the Lord, the God of Israel.
From the ends of the earth we hear songs of praise,
>>of glory to the Righteous One.—Isaiah 24:14-16

MEDITATION

Sacrifice culminates in praise. The self-emptying of Christ—
an inconceivable act of humility—leads ultimately to his
exaltation and that time when every knee shall bow and
every tongue confess that he is Lord. All of our acts of sacrifice end in acclaiming, "to the glory of thy blessed name."
The prophet Isaiah bears witness to the universal nature of
this doxology. The faithful shout from the west. They give
glory to the Lord in the east. The faithful lift their songs of
praise from the ends of the earth. Wesley masterfully par-
aphrases Psalm 150. The opening stanza of the hymn

enunciates the central theme of the Methodist revival: the God to whom we offer our praise is the God of love. Moreover, Wesley reveals that the effects of God's praise ripple more widely than any might imagine. Praising the holy God of love shows all God's greatness: "all" relating both to the vast dimensions of divine love and to the universal witness effected through the praise. When your life demonstrates the glory of God's blessed name, this act of praise proclaims to all around you the greatness of God's transforming love. The closing lines of the final stanza combine images from the Lord's Prayer and from David's Psalm of Praise. We proclaim God's holy name here below by giving our lives to Jesus, but by so doing, we join our voices to those of the faithful above who adore the God of love in eternal praise. Glory to God!

HYMN

This hymn can be sung to Amsterdam, the traditional setting for this hymn. Meter: 76.76.77.76

Praise the Lord who reigns above
    And keeps his court below;
Praise the holy God of love
    And all his greatness show!
Praise him for his noble deeds,
    Praise him for his matchless power;
Him from whom all good proceeds,
    Let earth and heaven adore.

God, in whom they move and live,
    Let every creature sing;
Glory to their Maker give,
    And homage to their King!

Hallowed be his name beneath,
  As in heaven on earth adored;
Praise the Lord in every breath;
  Let all things praise the Lord.

PRAYER

Gracious Lord, you sent your Word of truth and your Spirit of holiness to reveal the wondrous mystery of your love: grant me the grace to acknowledge the glory of your eternal Trinity and to adore the wonder of your everlasting Unity; hallowed be your name. Amen.

WEEK 20

I am not my own, but yours

SCRIPTURE

We do not live to ourselves, and we do not die to ourselves. If we live, we live to the Lord, and if we die, we die to the Lord; so then, whether we live or whether we die, we are the Lord's.—Romans 14:7-8

MEDITATION

A potent string of action verbs animates the remainder of this section of the prayer. After annunciating the covenant theme—"I am not my own, but yours"—Elizabeth prays for God to "claim me . . . , keep me . . . , love me. . . . Fight for me . . . , heal me . . . , and revive me. . . ." The opening words, drawn nearly verbatim from John Wesley's Covenant Prayer, set the tone for the rapid burst of supplications that follow. The petitions are intimate, urgent, and real: claim, keep, love, defend, heal, revive!

When we give ourselves to the Lord fully and freely, we can be assured that God will act. Moreover, the covenant act of surrender unites the believer to God in the most intimate of relationships, as the concluding words of Wesley's

Covenant Prayer demonstrate: "And now, O glorious and blessed God, Father, Son, and Holy Spirit, thou art mine, and I am thine. So be it. And the covenant which I have made on earth, let it be ratified in heaven." In his Gospel, John calls this *abiding*. Those who abide in God rest in the knowledge that the God of Promise cares.

The honesty and existential vigor of the supplications in Elizabeth's prayer demonstrate the security of children who know they are loved. Their heart's desire is to live to God's glory. Beloved children joy in rendering all to the One who has loved them so deeply. So profound are the consequences of this surrender that Paul claims, "whether we live or whether we die, we are the Lord's." Nothing in life means more than knowing you are Christ's.

HYMN

This hymn can be sung to Martyrdom, the tune used for "Alas! and Did My Savior Bleed." Meter: CM

> Let God to whom we now belong,
>   His sovereign right assert,
> And take up every thankful song,
>   And every loving heart.
>
> God justly claims us for his own
>   Who bought us with a price;
> The Christian lives to Christ alone,
>   To Christ alone one dies.
>
> Jesus, thine own at last receive!
>   Fulfil our heart's desire!
> And let us to thy glory live,
>   And in thy cause expire.

Our souls and bodies we resign:
    With joy we render thee
Our all, no longer ours, but thine
    To all eternity.

PRAYER

Gracious Lord, you have called me by my name and made me your own: grant me grace, therefore, to offer back my body and soul as a living sacrifice and to render to you all that I am, for I am no longer my own but yours throughout eternity, through Jesus Christ my Lord. Amen.

WEEK 21

Therefore claim me as your right

SCRIPTURE

Do you not know that all of us who have been baptized into Christ Jesus were baptized into his death? Therefore we have been buried with him by baptism into death, so that, just as Christ was raised from the dead by the glory of the Father, so we too might walk in newness of life.

For if we have been united with him in a death like his, we will certainly be united with him in a resurrection like his. We know that our old self was crucified with him so that the body of sin might be destroyed, and we might no longer be enslaved to sin. For whoever has died is freed from sin. But if we have died with Christ, we believe that we will also live with him.—Romans 6:3-8

MEDITATION

Have we become too fixated upon our rights? Unquestionably, the defense of human or inalienable rights has liberated many from the bondage of injustice throughout the world. But fixation upon personal rights can lead quite easily to the abandonment of responsibility. In such a situation, a spirit of entitlement emerges. "My right" becomes the measure of all things. A principle of radical autonomy feeds this narcissism that looks to "number one" in every question.

Standing almost in diametrical opposition to this distorted form of personal freedom, life in Christian community offers a strikingly different and alternative vision. For the Christian, "claim" is baptismal language. Rather than focusing on claims I think I can make about God or the importance of my rights in the marketplace of life, baptism reminds us about God's claim upon us and upon the community set apart as God's own. The baptized pray to God, "claim me as thy right." Is this not an unusual request for our day? Instead of making claims and demanding rights, we focus on the fact that we are already claimed, bought, in fact, at a costly price. Someone has a prior claim on us and a stake in us. We belong to God and to one another. That requires us to think and act differently about everything. It means dying to self. But it also means being united with Christ in his resurrection and plunging into the depths of God!

HYMN

This hymn can be sung to Stookey, the tune used for "O the Depth of Love Divine." Meter: 76.76.77.76

Father, Son, and Holy Ghost,
In solemn power come down!
Present with thy heavenly host,
Thine ordinance to crown.
See us, fallen here on earth!
Bless to us the cleansing flood!

Plunge us, by a second birth,
    Into the depths of God.

Let the promised inward grace
    Accompany the sign;
On our new-born souls impress
    The character divine!
Father, all thy love reveal!
    Jesus, all thy name impart!
Holy Ghost, renew and dwell
    For ever in our hearts!

PRAYER

Gracious Lord, God of new beginnings, you sent your Son into our midst to end the night of death with the new day of resurrection: Graft me so securely into the Living Vine through the sacrament of baptism that I may always give you thanks with a new and steadfast spirit. Amen.

WEEK 22

Keep me as your charge

SCRIPTURE

I call upon you, for you will answer me, O God;
      incline your ear to me, hear my words.
Wondrously show your steadfast love,
      O savior of those who seek refuge
      from their adversaries at your right hand.
Guard me as the apple of the eye;
      hide me in the shadow of your wings,
from the wicked who despoil me,
      my deadly enemies who surround me.

   . . . .

As for me, I shall behold your face in righteousness;
      when I awake I shall be satisfied, beholding your
         likeness.—Psalm 17:6-9, 15

MEDITATION

I love the novel *Lorna Doone*. In the story, Lorna discovers her true identity and learns that she is a ward of the state. That means the king of England literally has charge over her. He bears responsibility as her guardian. Elizabeth's prayer reminds me of that relationship when she prays, "keep me as your charge." She asks God to guard her life, to never let her go.

Perhaps this prayer found inspiration from an early hymn by Charles Wesley printed below. Using one of his typical literary devices, Wesley emphasizes the central theme by repeating the closing couplet in each stanza. "Keep me, keep me, gracious Lord, And never let me go." The One who keeps us raised us up, gave us back hope, consistently demonstrates loving-kindness. The Savior promises and delivers support and rest and never lets go. Those words, that universal appeal—"never let me go"— even found their way into the modern film adaptation of the *Titanic* saga. Often insecure and uncertain, feeling as though we are sinking to the depths, we seek reassurance that God will never let us go.

The Psalms express this theme repeatedly. In the portion of Psalm 17 quoted above, the seeker clings to the promise: I call, you will answer. I speak, you will listen. The subsequent images roll by quickly with great eloquence and power: keep me as the apple of your eye; hide me in the shadow of your wings. Keep me as your change and never let me go.

HYMN

This hymn can be sung to Amsterdam, the tune used for "Praise the Lord Who Reigns Above." Meter: 76.76.77.76

> Son of God, if thy free grace
>   Again hath raised me up,
> Called me still to seek thy face,
>   And given me back my hope;

Still thy timely help afford,
All thy loving-kindness show;
    Keep me, keep me, gracious Lord,
        And never let me go.

    Never let me leave thy breast,
        From thee, my Savior stray;
    Thou art my support and rest,
        My true and living way,
    My exceeding great reward,
In heaven above, and earth below:
    Keep me, keep me, gracious Lord,
        And never let me go.

PRAYER

Gracious Lord, you are my shelter against the burning heat of the day and the storms of life: help me when I stumble, catch me when I fall, and guide my steps firmly in faith toward the promise of eternal life, through Jesus Christ my Lord. Amen.

WEEK 23

And love me as your child

SCRIPTURE

See what love the Father has given us, that we should be called children of God; and that is what we are. The reason the world does not know us is that it did not know him. Beloved, we are God's children now; what we will be has not yet been revealed. What we do know is this: when he is revealed, we will be like him, for we will see him as he is. And all who have this hope in him purify themselves, just as he is pure. . . . The children of God and the children of the devil are revealed in this way: all who do not do what is right are not from God, nor are those who do not love their brothers and sisters. For this is the message you have heard from the beginning, that we should love one another.—1 John 3:1-3, 10-11

MEDITATION

There is a tender longing in this next petition: "love me as your child." No concern of the early Methodists consumed them more than the desire for every person to experience God's love and receive the assurance that she or he is a child of God. They knew all too well that many who came to their meetings for shelter, support, and encouragement had never experienced unconditional love from anyone. Through Christ, these Methodists discovered their true identity as beloved children of God, and they poured all their energy into making God's love real in their world. Having experienced the boundless love of God, they offered it freely to all.

John Wesley's translation of a German hymn by Paul Gerhardt celebrates this central mission of the Methodists. Essentially an extended prayer, the opening two stanzas consist of two fundamental petitions. The singer pleads for love to reign without rival in the heart. So many other forces in life compete to displace love from the center of our living, but God's love is the only reality worthy to fill that space. Then the singer pleads for total possession by love. Methodists yearn for the fullest possible love of God and neighbor and simply open their lives to the possibility of being more loving day by day. The Spirit takes it from there.

HYMN

This hymn can be sung to Saint Catherine, its traditional setting. Meter: 88.88.88

Jesu, thy boundless love to me
    No thought can reach, no tongue declare;
O knit my thankful heart to thee,
    And reign without a rival there!
Thine wholly, thine alone I am;
Be thou alone my constant flame!

O grant that nothing in my soul
    May dwell, but thy pure love alone!

O may thy love possess me whole,
   My joy, my treasure, and my crown;
Strange flames far from my heart remove—
My every act, word, thought, be love.

PRAYER

Gracious Lord, you love me as your own child and have prepared for those you love such good things as pass my understanding: pour into my heart such love for you that I, loving you above all things, may obtain your promises, which exceed all I could ever desire. Amen.

WEEK 24

Fight for me when I am assailed

SCRIPTURE

Moses said to the people, "Do not be afraid, stand firm, and see the deliverance that the LORD will accomplish for you today; for the Egyptians whom you see today you shall never see again. The LORD will fight for you, and you have only to keep still." Then the LORD said to Moses, "Why do you cry out to me? Tell the Israelites to go forward. But you lift up your staff, and stretch out your hand over the sea and divide it, that the Israelites may go into the sea on dry ground." . . . Thus the LORD saved Israel that day from the Egyptians.—Exodus 14:13-16, 30

MEDITATION

In the early years of Methodism, many who followed the Wesleys felt assailed in life by forces over which they had no control. Many were poor, barely able to eke out an existence through hard manual labor. Others, like the women who made up the majority of the movement, stood impotent on the margins of society. For those who felt overpowered, trapped, and forgotten, the event of the Exodus offered a vision of hope. It celebrated a God who was willing to fight for those beaten down by injustice and deprivation. At the very heart of the Exodus narrative, Moses declares, "The LORD will fight for you, and you have only to keep still." God stood on their side.

In "A Mighty Fortress Is Our God," Martin Luther depicts the evil perpetrated by the Prince of Darkness but exults in the promise of faith: "one little word shall fell him." Christ is that Word. Wesley's hymn, like Luther's, celebrates the One who fights for us when we are assailed. We fix our eyes on this Light. Guided by Christ, we have no fear of the ruin that surrounds us. Walking with him, not only are we able to survive the onslaught, but we actually become more than conquerors with him who wins his way. So we can rest. We only have to be still. The name of Jesus is our tower. The God of love—the great Deliverer of the people of God—remains ever faithful to us.

HYMN

Unusual Meter: 886.886

> Light of the world, thy beams I bless;
> On thee, bright Sun of righteousness,
> My faith hath fixed its eye;
> Guided by thee through all I go,
> Nor fear the ruin spread below,
> For thou art always nigh.
>
> Not all the powers of hell can fright
> A soul that walks with Christ in light;
> He walks, and cannot fall;
> Clearly he sees, and wins his way,

Shining unto the perfect day,
And more than conquers all.

I rest in thine almighty power;
The name of Jesus is a tower
That hides my life above!
Thou canst, thou wilt my helper be;
My confidence is all in thee,
The faithful God of love.

PRAYER

Gracious Lord, Guardian and Defender, as I travel through days filled with uncertainty: sustain me as I pass through the bitter valleys of suffering, shield me as dangers threaten, and let me rejoice in the springs of living water that refresh me on my way. Amen.

WEEK 25

Heal me when I am wounded

SCRIPTURE

For I will restore health to you,
    and your wounds I will heal,
            says the LORD,
because they have called you an outcast:
        "It is Zion; no one cares for her!"
Thus says the LORD:
I am going to restore the fortunes of the tents of Jacob,
        and have compassion on his dwellings;
the city shall be rebuilt upon its mound,
        and the citadel set on its rightful site.
Out of them shall come thanksgiving,
        and the sound of merrymakers.
I will make them many, and they shall not be few;
        I will make them honored, and they shall not be
            disdained.
Their children shall be as of old,
        their congregation shall be established before me;
        and I will punish all who oppress them.

Their prince shall be one of their own,
> their ruler shall come from their midst;
I will bring him near, and he shall approach me,
> for who would otherwise dare to approach me?
> > says the LORD.
And you shall be my people,
> and I will be your God.—Jeremiah 30:17-22

MEDITATION

When my family lived in Africa, it became clear to us almost immediately that African Christians closely associated their experience of God with healing. The healing stories of the Bible came to life as we heard the testimonies of our African friends. While the initial novelty of their testimony to healing related to differences of culture and worldview, increasingly we began to make connections with our Methodist heritage in unexpected ways.

Most Christians use the traditional language of forgiveness to describe salvation. Many Methodists, however, tend to add therapeutic imagery in expressing the purpose or goal of salvation. In the Wesleyan heritage, salvation relates to a process of restoration, the movement from brokenness to wholeness, the healing of wounds. Henri Nouwen wrote with eloquence about the call of Christians to be "wounded healers." All of us have sustained wounds; all of us have inflicted wounds. Life consists in large measure of a journey through grief and loss. Wounded, we cry out to God. We seek a balm to heal our wounds. We long for release from the discouragement that saps our energy and blinds us to all that is good and true in our lives. We yearn for wholeness and healing.

At a moment of deep despair, the Lord spoke through the prophet Jeremiah to God's people: "I will restore health to you, and your wounds I will heal." In the midst of your own helplessness, sickness, distress, and weariness, pray with Wesley: "let my soul, to health restored, Devote its little all to thee!"

HYMN

This hymn can be sung to Germany, the tune used for "Take Up Thy Cross." Meter: LM

O, God, to whom in flesh revealed
    The helpless all for succor came;
The sick to be relieved and healed,
    And found salvation in thy name.

Thou seest me helpless and distressed,
    Feeble, and faint, and blind, and poor:
Weary, I come to thee for rest,
    And sick of sin, implore a cure.

Be it according to thy word!
    Accomplish now thy work in me;
And let my soul, to health restored,
    Devote its little all to thee!

PRAYER

Gracious Lord, God of mercy and compassion, you hold out the hand of your mercy to raise me up and make me whole in the midst of my brokenness: though feeble and faint, poor and blind, in hope and trust I turn to you for healing, through Jesus Christ. Amen.

WEEK 26

And revive me when I am destroyed

SCRIPTURE

The joy of our hearts has ceased;
> our dancing has been turned to mourning.
The crown has fallen from our head;
> woe to us, for we have sinned!
Because of this our hearts are sick,
> because of these things our eyes have grown dim:
because of Mount Zion, which lies desolate;
> jackals prowl over it.

But you, O Lord, reign forever;
> your throne endures to all generations.
Why have you forgotten us completely?
> Why have you forsaken us these many days?
Restore us to yourself, O Lord,
> that we may be restored;
> renew our days as of old.—Lamentations 5:15-21

MEDITATION

Each petition in this prayer seems to grow in intensity. Often we need someone to fight for us. Wounds require healing. But this cry is more serious still. We require not only help and healing; our very survival depends upon resuscitation, because people and events in life destroy us. The petition moves beyond the hypothetical. There is no "if" here. "When" I am destroyed, the suppliant cries, only you can save me.

We turn to Lamentations for insight. The scene reflects our own worst nightmare. Hearts break. Dancing turns to mourning. The crown falls from the head. Eyes grow dim. Jackals prowl. Have you ever been there, destroyed and desolate? The despairing cry out to God, "Restore us to yourself, O LORD, that we may be restored!"

Charles Wesley published "And Are We Yet Alive" in 1749 at the close of one of the most difficult decades of the evangelical revival. Wesley had been run out of towns and stoned. Angry mobs threatened him repeatedly, and on more than one occasion he was lucky to escape with his life. What devastated Wesley the most was the fact that much of this resistance came from the leadership of the church he loved and served. But he continued to proclaim a message of love to those who despised him. This hymn is the third in a series of eight titled "At the Meeting of Friends." Whenever they "saw each other's face," they knew that God had saved them and preserved them from destruction!

HYMN

This hymn can be sung to Dennis, its traditional setting.
Meter: SM

> And are we yet alive,
> And see each other's face?
> Glory and praise to Jesus give
> For his redeeming grace!
>
> Preserved by power divine
> To full salvation here,
> Again in Jesu's praise we join,
> And in his sight appear.
>
> What troubles have we seen!
> What conflicts have we passed!
> Fightings without, and fears within,
> Since we assembled last.
> But out of all the Lord
> Hath brought us by his love;
> And still he doth his help afford,
> And hides our life above.

PRAYER

Gracious Lord, you are over all, in all, and beyond all: open my eyes to see your wonders and my lips to sing your praise, for you restore me in your image, who is Jesus Christ, your Son and my Lord, who reigns with you and the Holy Spirit, one God for ever and ever. Amen.

PART III

How does God shape my life?

My Lord and my God,
I ask you to give me patience in troubles, humility in comforts,
constancy in temptations, and victory over all my ghostly enemies.
Grant me sorrow for my sins, thankfulness for my benefits,
fear of your judgments, love of your mercies,
and mindfulness of your presence for evermore.
Make me humble to my superiors and friendly to my equals,
ready to please all and loathe to offend any;
loving to my friends and charitable to my enemies.
Give me modesty in my countenance,
gravity in my behavior, deliberation in my speech,
holiness in my thoughts, and righteousness in all my actions.
Let your mercy cleanse me from my sins,
and your grace bring forth in me the fruits of everlasting life.

WEEK 27

My Lord and my God, I ask you to give me patience in troubles, humility in comforts

SCRIPTURE

For this reason, since the day we heard it, we have not ceased praying for you and asking that you may be filled with the knowledge of God's will in all spiritual wisdom and under-standing, so that you may lead lives worthy of the Lord, fully pleasing to him, as you bear fruit in every good work and as you grow in the knowledge of God. May you be made strong with all the strength that comes from his glorious power, and may you be prepared to endure everything with patience while joyfully giving thanks to the Father, who has enabled you to share in the inheritance of the saints in the light. He has rescued us from the power of darkness and transferred us into the kingdom of his beloved Son.—Colossians 1:9-13

MEDITATION

It is important to ask repeatedly, *How does God shape my life?* Certainly, practices, people, and events all form us—we hope more fully into the image of Christ. Experiences in community often exert a more profound influence upon us than we realize. God uses personal disciplines and communal practices to conform our hearts, minds, and actions to the true humanity revealed in Christ Jesus. The third section of our life-shaping prayer opens with Thomas's acclamation: "My Lord and my God!" (John 20:28). The personal pronouns reflect the intimate nature of the apostle's confession. In the preceding twenty-six weeks I have focused the tone of these meditations more on the "we" than the "I." But in our journey of faith it is sometimes difficult to know where the "I" ends and the "we" begins. In the confession of Thomas, however, faith acquires an emphatic quality. Like the collects that conclude each week, all voiced in the most personal language, "the" faith becomes "my" own.

The two stanzas of this week's hymn come from a much larger poetic work on the love feast by Charles Wesley. The Wesley brothers developed a communal meal called the love feast in the hope that the Spirit would use these gatherings to shape disciples into whole and happy children of God. Love feasts cultivated virtue, nurtured the fruit of the Spirit, and, most importantly, signaled love as the most precious gift of all. Patience and humility, highlighted in our prayer today, figure prominently among all virtues because they reflect most fully the mind that was in Christ.

HYMN

This hymn can be sung to Messiah, the tune used for "Take My Life, and Let It Be." Meter: 77.77 D

> Let the fruits of grace abound,
> Let in us thy mercies sound;
> Faith, and love, and joy increase,

Temperance and gentleness;
Plant in us thy humble mind,
Patient, pitiful, and kind;
Meek and lowly let us be
Full of goodness, full of thee.

Make us all in thee complete,
Make us all for glory meet,
Meet t'appear before thy sight,
Partners with the saints in light.
Call, O call us each by name
To the marriage of the Lamb;
Let us lean upon thy breast!
Love be there our endless feast!

PRAYER

Gracious Lord, you will for me to give thanks in everything, to fear nothing but the loss of you, and to use my gifts for your glory: free me from faithless fears and anxieties that blind me to your calling, and give me patience to run my course with perseverance. Amen.

WEEK 28

Constancy in temptations, and victory over all my ghostly enemies

SCRIPTURE

Jesus, full of the Holy Spirit, returned from the Jordan and was led by the Spirit in the wilderness, where for forty days he was tempted by the devil. He ate nothing at all during those days, and when they were over, he was famished. The devil said to him, "If you are the Son of God, command this stone to become a loaf of bread." Jesus answered him, "It is written, 'One does not live by bread alone.'" Then the devil led him up and showed him in an instant all the kingdoms of the world. And the devil said to him, "To you I will give their glory and all this authority; for it has been given over to me, and I give it to anyone I please. If you, then, will worship me, it will all be yours." Jesus answered him, "It is written, 'Worship the Lord your God, and serve only him.'" Then the devil took him to Jerusalem, and placed him on the pinnacle of the temple, saying to him, "If you are the Son of God, throw yourself down from here, for it is written, 'He will command his angels concerning you, to protect you,' and 'On their hands they will bear you up, so that you will not dash your foot against a stone.'" Jesus answered him, "It is said, 'Do not put the Lord your God to the test.'" When the devil had finished every test, he departed from him until an opportune time.—Luke 4:1-13

MEDITATION

As we open ourselves to the shaping influence of the Holy Spirit, we must remember, as Charles Wesley wrote, that we are "feeble, tempted followers here"! As a wise colleague once told me, "Recognize and accept your limitations." We like to believe that we control our own destiny. We want to be in charge. Our failure to recognize our weaknesses and vulnerabilities opens the door to temptation's seductive power. Only God can sustain us through times of temptation. Wesley reminds us that whenever the water threatens to overwhelm us, Jesus appears on the flood. When passing through fire, we feel Jesus present in the flame. Our hope rests in him, who was tempted in every way just as we are, but always kept his face fixed upon God and God's way.

Jesus' constancy delivers us from all the subtle and blatant entrapments of evil. *Temptation* remains one of my favorite works from the pen of the German theologian Dietrich Bonhoeffer. He delivered these brief lectures in April 1937 to a group of clergy in the Confessing Church who faced possible martyrdom because of their opposition of the Nazis. Bonhoeffer realized that temptation robs the Christian of staying power. The story of Jesus' own temptation demonstrates his dependence on the saving, enduring Word of God. Because Jesus was tempted, we need no longer confront temptation alone. To share in Christ's atoning life means that we share his triumph as well. Knowing that he has won the victory, that we are not tempted alone, gives us the help we need.

HYMN

This hymn can be sung to Saint Petersburg, the tune used for "Thou Hidden Source of Calm Repose." Meter: 88.88.88

Jesu, to thee our hearts we lift,
    May all our hearts with love o'erflow
With thanks for thy continued gift
    That still thy precious name we know,
Retain our sense of sin forgiven,
And wait for all our inward heaven.

What mighty troubles hast thou shown
    Thy feeble, tempted followers here!
We have through fire and water gone,
    But saw thee on the floods appear;
But felt thee present in the flame,
And shouted our Deliverer's name.

Thou, who hast kept us to this hour,
    O keep us faithful to the end!
When, robed with majesty and power,
    Our Jesus shall from heaven descend,
His friends and confessors to own,
And seat us on his glorious throne.

PRAYER

Gracious Lord, when you were led by the Spirit to be tempted in the wilderness, you demonstrated your power over the forces of evil: knowing my weaknesses as you do, come quickly to my aid whenever I am tempted to follow a road that is contrary to your way. Amen.

WEEK 29

Grant me sorrow for my sins, thankfulness for my benefits

SCRIPTURE

But when he came to himself he said, "How many of my father's hired hands have bread enough and to spare, but here I am dying of hunger! I will get up and go to my father, and I will say to him, 'Father, I have sinned against heaven and before you; I am no longer worthy to be called your son; treat me like one of your hired hands.'" So he set off and went to his father. But while he was still far off, his father saw him and was filled with compassion; he ran and put his arms around him and kissed him. Then the son said to him, "Father, I have sinned against heaven and before you; I am no longer worthy to be called your son." But the father said to his slaves, "Quickly, bring out a robe—the best one—and put it on him; put a ring on his finger and sandals on his feet. And get the fatted calf and kill it, and let us eat and celebrate; for this son of mine was dead and is alive again; he was lost and is found!" And they began to celebrate.—Luke 15:17-24

MEDITATION

The next three petitions of the prayer are intimately connected to the Wesleyan way of salvation. On one occasion, when asked about the essential doctrines of the Methodists, John Wesley summarized their vision of redemption in three words: *repentance, faith,* and *holiness*. The readings for today focus attention upon repentance as the "porch" of religion, the threshold that leads to a vital relationship with God through Christ.

No narrative of the New Testament provides greater insight into the nature of repentance than the parable of the prodigal son. Having squandered his inheritance, the younger of two sons is overcome with remorse. We pick up the story in the passage from Luke's Gospel at the most critical moment. The Evangelist encapsulates the turning point of the prodigal's life in the words, "But when he came to himself." The Wesleys defined repentance as "true self-understanding." This unique definition consists of two critical insights: first, the sinner recognizes how far he or she is from God's purpose and intention; second, like the prodigal, the broken and fallen realize that their true home is with the father—they are children of God. True repentance is the product, not the premise, of Jesus' presence.

The hymn from the Wesleys' 1739 *Hymns and Sacred Poems* reflects the urgent nature of repentance in the biblical story. In the opening stanza the "lost and undone" sinner flees to Jesus, the sinner's friend. The successive stanzas elevate a vision of salvation as healing, homecoming, and holiness rooted in the free offer of the self to Christ, who alone can save.

HYMN

This hymn can be sung to Wareham, the tune used for "O Wondrous Sight! O Vision Fair." Meter: LM

Jesu, the sinner's friend, to thee,
Lost and undone for aid I flee,
Weary of earth, myself, and sin—
Open thine arms, and take me in.

Pity, and heal my sin-sick soul;
'Tis thou alone canst make me whole,
Fallen, till in me thine image shine,
And cursed I am, till thou art mine.

The mansion for thyself prepare
Dispose my heart by entering there;
'Tis this alone can make me clean,
'Tis this alone can cast out sin.

At last I own it cannot be
That I should fit myself for thee;
Here then to thee I all resign—
Thine is the work, and only thine.

PRAYER

Gracious Lord, all my sins are known to you and all my ugly ways are clear before you: have mercy on me, have mercy on me in my pitiful attempts to hide my sin behind the pretense of holiness, and grant me the joy that comes from true self-knowledge and full repentance. Amen.

WEEK 30

Fear of your judgments, love of your mercies

SCRIPTURE

Out of the depths I cry to you, O LORD.
Lord, hear my voice!
Let your ears be attentive
to the voice of my supplications!

If you, O LORD, should mark iniquities,
      Lord, who could stand?
But there is forgiveness with you,
        so that you may be revered.

I wait for the LORD, my soul waits,
      and in his word I hope;
my soul waits for the Lord
more than those who watch for the morning,
      more than those who watch for the morning.

O Israel, hope in the LORD!
      For with the LORD there is steadfast love,
and with him is great power to redeem.
It is he who will redeem Israel
      from all its iniquities.—Psalm 130

MEDITATION

The repentant sinner, who turns to the Lord "out of the depths," waits in hope for a word of salvation from the God of steadfast love. Charles Wesley's paraphrase of Psalm 130 explores the pathos of supplication and expectation in the child of God awakened to his or her true identity. Those who do not resist God's presence realize that there is nothing they can do to heal themselves or restore the relationships that bring meaning to life. They despair of self and place their hope in God, entrusting their lives fully to Christ. Forgiveness leads to adoration. As the psalmist expresses it, "there is forgiveness with you, so that you may be revered." Those grieved by alienation from God yearn to see God's "lovely face," expecting God's grace and resting in God's promise.

In the closing stanza of the hymn, Wesley compares God's forgiveness received by faith with the dawn of the morning light. "O that his mercy's beams would rise, And bring the Gospel-day!" he sings. For those who put their trust in the Lord, "great power to redeem" awaits. Overwhelming joy displaces the fear of judgment; but the fear of the Lord—the sense of awe—remains as an awareness of God's steadfast mercy. God longs to embrace and make new. Wait for the Lord in trusting faith, for with the Lord there is steadfast love. When you cry out of the depths, God will hear your voice and respond with grace and mercy and love.

HYMN

This hymn can be sung to Morning Song, the tune used for "My Soul Gives Glory to My God." Meter: CM

> Out of the depth of self-despair
> > To thee, O Lord, I cry;
> My misery mark, attend my prayer,
> > And bring salvation nigh.
>
> O Lord! Forgiveness is with thee,
> > That sinners may adore,
> With filial fear thy goodness see,
> > And never grieve thee more.
>
> I look to see his lovely face,
> > I wait to meet my Lord,
> My longing soul expects his grace,
> > And rests upon his word.
>
> My soul, while still to him it flies,
> > Prevents the morning ray;
> O that his mercy's beams would rise,
> > And bring the Gospel-day!

PRAYER

Gracious Lord, hope of Israel and joy of the redeemed: hear me when I cry to you out of the depths, for I long to see your face and to receive your grace as I rest in your Word of promise, even the Christ who lives and reigns with you and the Holy Spirit, one God forever more. Amen.

WEEK 31

And mindfulness of your presence for evermore

SCRIPTURE

Where can I go from your spirit?
 Or where can I flee from your presence?
If I ascend to heaven, you are there;
 if I make my bed in Sheol, you are there.
If I take the wings of the morning
 and settle at the farthest limits of the sea,
even there your hand shall lead me,
 and your right hand shall hold me fast.

—Psalm 139:7-10

MEDITATION

One of the most important spiritual mentors in my life, Brother Mark Gibbard, suggested that I meditate on Psalm 139 every morning for a month. He predicted the experience would change my life. The particular portion of the psalm that continues to inspire me more than any other is the reading for today. It opens with those amazing words: "Where can I go from your spirit?" Most people, I think, initially respond to this passage in a negative rather than a positive way. "You mean I can never escape God?" they might ask.

John Wesley's adaptation of Isaac Watts's paraphrase of the psalm turns this question around to ask, *Why would anyone want to flee from this "wondrous Knowledge"?* Notice how he turns every image into a reason for celebration. Why hide when "within thy circling arms I lie"? If I fly beyond the West, it is God's hand that supports my flight. God's grace surrounds us, an ever-present bulwark to guard the soul and fill it with love.

Brother Lawrence wrote about practicing the presence of God. Rather than fear God's presence, he *practiced* it. He reminded himself daily of the love that surrounded him. He rested in the knowledge that he would never be alone. The goal of the Christian life is to welcome that presence, live in that love, and radiate this loving presence in all we do. Abiding in the presence of God sustains love for God and others. This is the goal of all true religion; we call it holiness.

HYMN

This hymn can be sung to Saint Peter, the tune used for "Where Charity and Love Prevail." Meter: CM

Lord, all I am is known to thee,
   In vain my soul would try
To shun thy presence, or to flee
   The notice of thine eye.

O wondrous Knowledge, deep and high!
   Where can a creature hide?
Within thy circling arms I lie
   Beset on every side.

If winged with beams of morning light,
    I fly beyond the west,
Thy hand, which must support my flight,
    Would soon betray my rest.

So let thy grace surround me still,
    And like a bulwark prove,
To guard my soul from every ill,
    Secured by sov'reign love.

PRAYER

Gracious Lord, where can I go from your Spirit or flee from your presence, for you are everywhere? Help me to receive this word not as a curse but as an amazing blessing, for you promise to lead me by your hand and hold me in your arms as your beloved child. Amen.

WEEK 32

Make me humble to my superiors and friendly to my equals

SCRIPTURE

For by the grace given to me I say to everyone among you not to think of yourself more highly than you ought to think, but to think with sober judgment, each according to the measure of faith that God has assigned. For as in one body we have many members, and not all the members have the same function, so we, who are many, are one body in Christ, and individually we are members one of another.—Romans 12:3-5

MEDITATION

Faithful Christian disciples practice life in community. Paul uses the image of the body of Christ repeatedly to teach this lesson.

Nothing cultivates the virtue of humility and appreciation for others more fully than family life. Joined together by the grace of God, Christians learn how to love in the context of God's family. If Christ stands at the center of life together, with everyone moving toward him and seeking to live the way of Jesus, then all move closer to one another.

Charles Wesley describes this path to peace and harmony in the opening stanza of the hymn below. Powerful images depict the nature of Christian community. We are gathered into one, build each other up, and go on hand in hand. We move together toward "our high calling's glorious hope"—namely, the same unity manifest in the Three-One God. Jesus even prays that we might be one as he and the Father are one. The stanzas that follow elevate two of God's most important gifts: grace and peace. God surrounds every person with grace, excluding none. In the body of Christ, God's gracious activity makes it possible for every person to become a vessel through which God's immeasurable love flows. Reconciling, healing, restoring love unites the body and bears witness to God's presence in the world. In such a community, we not only experience peace as a personal gift; everyone feels a "common peace." Bound together in grace as instruments of God's love, we offer "joy unspeakable" to the world.

HYMN

This hymn can be sung to Armenia, its traditional setting. Meter: CM

> All praise to our redeeming Lord,
>   Who joins us by his grace,
> And bids us, each to each restored,
>   Together seek his face.
>
> Christ bids us build each other up;
>   And, gathered into one,

To our high calling's glorious hope
    We hand in hand go on.

The gift which he on one bestows,
    We all delight to prove,
The grace through every vessel flows
    In purest streams of love.

We all partake the joy of one;
    The common peace we feel,
A peace to sensual minds unknown,
    A joy unspeakable.

PRAYER

Gracious Lord, who assigns to all a measure of faith and gifts to be used in the realization of your peaceable rule in the world: guard me from thinking about myself more highly than I ought and bind me together with my brothers and sisters as in one family, through Christ. Amen.

WEEK 33

Ready to please all and loathe to offend any

SCRIPTURE

For though I am free with respect to all, I have made myself a slave to all, so that I might win more of them. To the Jews I became as a Jew, in order to win Jews. To those under the law I became as one under the law (though I myself am not under the law) so that I might win those under the law. To those outside the law I became as one outside the law (though I am not free from God's law but am under Christ's law) so that I might win those outside the law. To the weak I became weak, so that I might win the weak. I have become all things to all people, that I might by all means save some. I do it all for the sake of the gospel, so that I may share in its blessings.—1 Corinthians 9:19-23

MEDITATION

Hospitality relates to the ability to make others feel comfortable and accepted. In a study entitled *Making Room: Recovering Hospitality as a Christian Tradition*, Christine Pohl demonstrates the centrality of this practice in Christian discipleship. Paul describes this attitude in terms of becoming all things to all people. Far from a chameleonlike existence in which we change our colors to accommodate, concern focuses on the "other" and not ourselves. Hospitality is about making connections with people and caring genuinely for others, particularly for those left out.

No hymn embodies this welcoming vision better than "Come, Sinners, to the Gospel Feast." Based on the parable of the great banquet in Luke 14, Charles Wesley first published this lengthy hymn of twenty-four stanzas in his 1747 collection of *Redemption Hymns*. The Lord's Table functions in the hymn as a paradigm of welcome, inclusion, and winsome love. God extends the invitation to all to join together at the Table and desires that none be left behind. In Jesus' own table fellowship practices, those with whom he sought to eat were often the last any expected. He demonstrated his concern to the broken, the marginalized, the lonely, and the insignificant in the eyes of the world. He turned the order of the world upside down as the poor gathered around his table to share in food and fellowship with him. God invites those oppressed by sin; those who wander restlessly through life; those who face emotional and physical challenges every day. God identifies with these persons. Christ makes room for you!

HYMN

This hymn can be sung to Hursley, its traditional setting. Meter: LM

> Come, sinners, to the gospel feast;
>> Let every soul be Jesu's guest;
> Ye need not one be left behind,
>> For God hath bid all humankind.

Sent by my Lord, on you I call;
    The invitation is to all:
Come, all the world; Come, sinner, thou!
All things in Christ are ready now.

Come, all ye souls by sin oppressed,
    Ye restless wanderers after rest;
Ye poor, and maimed, and halt, and blind,
    In Christ a hearty welcome find.

This is the time: no more delay!
    This is the Lord's accepted day;
Come thou, this moment, at his call,
    And live for him who died for all!

PRAYER

Gracious Lord, who called your church to witness that you were in Christ reconciling all people to yourself: gather all of your children around your table for the gospel feast and shape me in such a way by your Spirit that your invitation might be extended to all through me. Amen.

WEEK 34

Loving to my friends and charitable to my enemies

SCRIPTURE

You have heard that it was said, "You shall love your neighbor and hate your enemy." But I say to you, Love your enemies and pray for those who persecute you, so that you may be children of your Father in heaven; for he makes his sun rise on the evil and on the good, and sends rain on the righteous and on the unrighteous. For if you love those who love you, what reward do you have? Do not even the tax collectors do the same? And if you greet only your brothers and sisters, what more are you doing than others? Do not even the Gentiles do the same? Be perfect, therefore, as your heavenly Father is perfect.—Matthew 5:43-48

MEDITATION

God shapes us by our life together in the body of Christ—the church—and by the Table fellowship of God's family. God also forms our spirits through our practice of love. Loving those who are close to us, and for whom love comes somewhat naturally, will always remain significant. But nothing refashions our souls more than the effort—the gift—of loving those who are most unlovable. Jesus made this clear in his Sermon on the Mount. In this regard, he even went so far as to say that the love of our enemies demonstrates the fullest possible love in our lives. God loves like this; through Christ we can love this way too.

The words of the seventeenth-century poet Samuel Crossman capture the essence of this love and the motivation that stands behind it:

> My song is love unknown;
> My Savior's love to me;
> Love to the loveless shown,
> That they might lovely be.
> O who am I
>> That for my sake,
>> My Lord should take
> Frail flesh, and die?

God awakens this love in us when we permit Christ to take full possession of our souls, when we allow the Spirit to form his character completely in our lives. Such a restoration, such a transformation takes time, but is God's greatest gift. To become perfect as God is perfect is to love with this kind of love. And when we do, it sparkles from within, wills that all should live, and prevails in every situation: "Love immense, and unconfined, Love to all of humankind."

HYMN
This hymn can be sung to Dix, used for "For the Beauty of the Earth." Meter: 77.77.77

> Come, thou holy God and true!
> Come, and my whole heart renew;

Take me now, possess me whole,
Form the Savior of my soul:
    Love immense, and unconfined,
    Love to all of humankind.

Happy soul, whose active love
Emulates the Blessed above,
In thy every action seen,
Sparkling from the soul within:
    Love immense, and unconfined,
    Love to all of humankind.

Love, which willest all should live,
Love, which all to all would give,
Love, that over all prevails,
Love, that never, never fails:
    Love immense, and unconfined,
    Love to all of humankind.

PRAYER

Gracious Lord, Love immense and unconfined, you have taught me that without love nothing I do has any worth: through the power of your Holy Spirit pour the great gift of love into my heart that I might offer it freely to all for the sake of your only Son Jesus Christ. Amen.

WEEK 35

Give me modesty in my countenance

SCRIPTURE

The wisdom of a humble man will lift up his head, and will seat him among the great. Do not praise a man for his good looks, nor loathe a man because of his appearance. The bee is small among flying creatures, but her product is the best of sweet things. Do not boast about wearing fine clothes, nor exalt yourself in the day that you are honored; for the works of the Lord are wonderful, and his works are concealed from men. Many kings have had to sit on the ground, but one who was never thought of has worn a crown.—Sirach 11:1-5

MEDITATION

The author of Sirach served as a teacher of Jewish law in the second century BCE. The book in the Apocrypha that bears his name reflects a tradition stretching back to the ancient sayings in Proverbs. Sirach, or Ecclesiasticus, the last work of a collection of writings known as Hebrew wisdom literature, inspired the Wesleys and shaped Methodist discipleship.

Charles Wesley particularly appreciated the way Sirach wove his proverbial sayings into a poetic framework. The themes of this week's reading and the next bear a striking resemblance to this tradition of wisdom. Today's reading elevates modesty and simplicity. Sirach uses two particularly poignant images. First, the bee is a tiny insect, but the product of her labor is exceedingly sweet. She fulfills her role by virtue of her focus and simplicity. Second, verse five is a potent reminder about the order of things in God's reign. While many kings will sit on the ground, the one never considered great wins the crown. The message is clear: God elevates those who are modest, simple, and singular of heart.

The singer of Wesley's hymn prays for true simplicity. Knowing God supersedes all other achievements in life. We can be carried away so easily by our own knowledge and pride. Rather than boasting in our own wisdom, we need to become teachable and docile like children. To be shaped into a true disciple of Christ means to focus on his light and to walk in his simple path of love.

HYMN

This hymn can be sung to The Call, the tune used for "Come, My Way, My Truth, My Life." Meter: 77.77

Lord, that I may learn of thee,
Give me true simplicity;
Wean my soul, and keep it low,
Willing thee alone to know.

Let me cast my reeds aside,
All that feeds my knowing pride,
Not to self, but God submit,
Lay my reasonings at thy feet.

Of my boasted wisdom spoiled,
Docile, helpless as a child,
Only seeing in thy light,
Only walking in thy might.

Then infuse the teaching grace,
Spirit of truth and righteousness;
Knowledge, love divine impart,
Life eternal to my heart.

PRAYER

Gracious Lord, whose power lies in weakness and whose wisdom confounds the wise: give me simplicity of heart and mind, make me docile like a child, teachable and open to the knowledge that comes only from you, that Christ might reign without rival in my heart. Amen.

WEEK 36

Gravity in my behavior, deliberation in my speech

SCRIPTURE

Do nothing without deliberation; and when you have acted, do not regret it. Do not go on a path full of hazards, and do not stumble over stony ground. Do not be overconfident on a smooth way, and give good heed to your paths. Guard yourself in every act, for this is the keeping of the commandments. He who believes the law gives heed to the commandments, and he who trusts the Lord will not suffer loss.—Sirach 32:19-24, RSV

MEDITATION

God must shape the "well-instructed soul." Many qualities characterize a person who has been taught by God, but perhaps no two traits are more important than gravity and deliberation. Persons with gravitas exhibit well-thought-out action. Their decisions, we might say, are weighty; their behavior is anchored, down to earth, solid. Not only do they think through their actions carefully, but their speech exhibits the same intentionality. They are careful about how they say things and when they speak. They measure their words. Truth characterizes their words; their actions are transparent. The conscience guards and guides the words and actions of a well-instructed soul.

The original title of Wesley's hymn for today was "For a Tender Conscience." He understood the importance of an internal guidance mechanism—a principle within—that functions as an arbiter of words and actions. He knew the importance of cultivating the conscience to maintenance of healthy and happy relationships. Most importantly, he was concerned that the early Methodist people develop a biblical understanding of how good and evil forces shape decisions in our lives. Of particular concern to him was the seductive power of pride, wrong desire, and the wandering will.

Permitting God to shape our lives means bringing unruly wills and passions under the control of a godly principle. It means fixing this principle at the very center of our being, the source of all words and actions. It means testing every thought, word, and deed against the measure of God's love.

HYMN

This hymn can be sung to Gerald, its traditional setting. Meter: CMD

> I want a principle within
> Of jealous, godly fear,
> A sensibility of sin,
> A pain to feel it near.

> If to the right or left I stray,
> That moment, Lord, reprove,
> And let me weep my life away
> For having grieved thy love.

O may the least omission pain
    My well-instructed soul,
And drive me to the blood again
    Which makes the wounded whole.

PRAYER

Gracious Lord, you alone can bring order to the unruly wills and passions of your children: establish within me a fixed principle, both a spiritual sensitivity and a spirit of deliberation, that I might love what you command and desire what you promise. Amen.

WEEK 37

Holiness in my thoughts, and righteousness in all my actions

SCRIPTURE

Beloved, since God loved us so much, we also ought to love one another. No one has ever seen God; if we love one another, God lives in us, and his love is perfected in us. . . . So we have known and believe the love God has for us. God is love, and those who abide in love abide in God, and God abides in them. Love has been perfected among us in this: that we may have boldness on the day of judgment, because as he is, so are we in this world. There is no fear in love, but perfect love casts out fear; for fear has to do with punishment, and whoever fears has not reached perfection in love. We love because he first loved us. Those who say, "I love God," and hate their brothers or sisters, are liars; for those who do not love a brother or sister whom they have seen, cannot love God whom they have not seen. The commandment we have from him is this: those who love God must love their brothers and sisters also.—1 John 4:11-12, 16-21

MEDITATION

Humility, hospitality, and loving-kindness; simplicity and deliberation—all are God-shaped qualities of life. To have all the mind that was in Christ, however, means that these qualities flow from Christ's holiness and righteousness in us through loving actions toward others. God not only attributes righteousness to us, but God imparts it as well. Not only are we declared good and pure on the basis of Christ's redemptive work for us, but the Spirit recreates us in such a way that true righteousness and holiness characterize the way we live.

We grow into this new being in Christ only because the indwelling Spirit of God influences us. The faithful disciple of Christ is apt to find a tension between this new principle (considered in the last week's meditation) and the remains of obstinate rebellion against God's way. As Martin Luther once observed, God drowns the old Adam through the sacrament of baptism, but he is a very good swimmer. The gift of perfect love, however, releases the believer from that tension and enables all the energies of a child of God to flow in the direction of love to God and neighbor.

Reflecting on two texts from Genesis, Charles Wesley articulates this vision of the Christian life. Everything begins with God's all-sufficient grace. We can only experience purity of heart and life—holiness and righteousness—as a consequence of God's gracious gift. "Through faith begotten from above," we are "stamped with real holiness," claims Wesley, "All filled with perfect love!"

HYMN

This hymn can be sung to Amsterdam, the tune used for "Praise the Lord Who Reigns Above." Meter: 76.76.78.76

> God of all-sufficient grace,
>> My God in Christ thou art;
> Bid me walk before thy face
>> Till I am pure in heart;
> Till, transformed by faith divine,
> I gain that perfect love unknown,
>> Bright in all thy image shine,
>>> By putting on thy Son.
>
> Father, Son, and Holy Ghost,
>> In council join anew
> To retrieve what Adam lost,
>> Thine image to renew;
> O might I thy form express,
> Through faith begotten from above,
>> Stamped with real holiness,
>>> And filled with perfect love!

PRAYER

Gracious Lord, God of all-sufficient grace, whose will is that all might love as they have been loved in Christ: stamp your image upon my soul, restore your loving character in my spirit, and refashion my whole being into a transcript of your holiness in both heart and life. Amen.

WEEK 38

Let your mercy cleanse me from my sins

SCRIPTURE

Have mercy on me, O God,
>according to your steadfast love; according to
your abundant mercy
>blot out my transgressions.
Wash me thoroughly from my iniquity,
>and cleanse me from my sin.

For I know my transgressions,
>and my sin is ever before me.
Against you, you alone, have I sinned,
>and done what is evil in your sight,
so that you are justified in your sentence
>and blameless when you pass judgment.

> . . . .

Create in me a clean heart, O God,
>and put a new and right spirit within me.
Do not cast me away from your presence,
>and do not take your holy spirit from me.
>>—Psalm 51:1-4, 10-11

MEDITATION

Jonathan Coussins, the author of Elizabeth's prayer, immediately juxtaposes his plea for holiness and righteousness with a potent reminder that we can easily twist God's gifts into our own achievements. We deceive ourselves whenever we forget that universal prayer: *Kyrie eleison*—Lord, have mercy. While a sense of achievement can make us feel that we have put sin behind us for good, gratitude for the gift of perfect love reminds us perennially that we are always in need of God's forgiveness through Christ.

Wesley's eight-stanza poem entitled "Make Me a Clean Heart, O God" reflects upon the familiar tenth verse of Psalm 51: "Create in me a clean heart, O God, and put a new and right spirit within me." The Wesleys prayed this prayer every day in their morning devotions. The opening verse of the psalm sets the tone of this meditative song: "Have mercy on me, O God, according to your steadfast love; according to your abundant mercy blot out my transgressions." Only God's grace can sustain this reciprocal love in our hearts.

To claim that I have a pure heart is the height of presumption. All I can do is pray for God to grant me a heart that loves as Christ has loved me. Wesley describes the heart cleansed of sin and filled with love. It is renewed in every way: perfect, right, pure, good—"a copy" of the heart of Jesus. Impart your very nature to me, he prays. Write your new, best name of love, Lord Jesus, on my heart.

HYMN

This hymn can be sung to Richmond, its traditional setting.
Meter: CM

O for a heart to praise my God,
    A heart from sin set free!
A heart that always feels thy blood,
    So freely spilt for me!

A heart in every thought renewed,
    And full of love divine,
Perfect, and right, and pure, and good—
    A copy, Lord, of thine!

Thy nature, gracious Lord, impart;
    Come quickly from above;
Write thy new name upon my heart,
    Thy new, best name of love!

PRAYER

Gracious Lord, O God and giver of all good gifts, you cleanse me from the stain and sin and make me pure of heart through the death and resurrection of your Son: grant me grace to live in gratitude and to dwell with you in true holiness of heart and life. Amen.

WEEK 39

And your grace bring forth in me the fruits of everlasting life

SCRIPTURE

For I handed on to you as of first importance what I in turn had received: that Christ died for our sins in accordance with the scriptures, and that he was buried, and that he was raised on the third day in accordance with the scriptures. . . . If for this life only we have hoped in Christ, we are of all people most to be pitied. But in fact Christ has been raised from the dead, the first fruits of those who have died. For since death came through a human being, the resurrection of the dead has also come through a human being; for as all die in Adam, so all will be made alive in Christ. But each in his own order: Christ the first fruits, then at his coming those who belong to Christ.—1 Corinthians 15:3-4, 19-23

MEDITATION

Among all the ways God shapes our lives, perhaps none is so important as the way the Spirit prepares us for eternal life with God. In the fifteenth chapter of his first letter to the

Corinthians, Paul reflects upon the centrality of Christ's resurrection and celebrates God's gift of resurrection for each of us through him. The end of faith, just like its beginning, is rooted in grace. Only God's grace can bring forth this ultimate fruit in our lives. All of life prepares us for this ultimate gift, to dwell eternally with the God of love.

Certainly, my grandfather was right when he told me repeatedly, "It takes a lifetime to learn how to live." But this lifetime of formation prepares us for the homecoming for which we were created.

We find the end in the beginning in one of Charles Wesley's most famous hymns, "Hark! the Herald Angels Sing." We most fully understand the birth of Christ when we comprehend the purpose of his advent in our lives. The third stanza of the hymn explicitly describes God's design. Christ is born that we no more may die. Christ is born to raise us from the earth. Christ is born to give us second birth. A seldom-sung stanza of this familiar carol further elaborates the work of Christ. Through Christ, God restores our nature. God unites us mystically with Christ. God comes down to us in Christ. The Spirit elevates us to the fullness of eternal life in him.

HYMN

This hymn can be sung to Mendelssohn, the traditional setting for this hymn. Meter: 77.77 D with Refrain

> Christ, by highest heaven adored;
>   Christ, the everlasting Lord;
> Late in time behold him come,
>   Offspring of a virgin's womb.
> Veiled in flesh the Godhead see;
>   Hail the incarnate Deity,

Pleased with us in flesh to dwell,
    Jesus, our Emmanuel.

    Refrain: Hark! the herald angels sing,
        "Glory to the newborn King."

Hail the heaven-born Prince of Peace!
    Hail the Sun of Righteousness!
Light and life to all he brings,
    Risen with healing in his wings.
Mild he lays his glory by,
    Born that we no more may die,
Born to raise us from the earth,
    Born to give us second birth.   Refrain

Now display thy saving power,
    Ruined nature now restore,
Now in mystic union join
    Thine to ours, and ours to thine.
Adam's likeness, Lord, efface,
    Stamp thine image in its place,
Second Adam from above,
    Reinstate us in thy love!   Refrain

PRAYER

Gracious Lord, through the death and resurrection of your Son you overcame death and brought forth the first fruits of everlasting life: grant that I may be raised from death and restored to newness of life through Jesus, my Lord, who rose with healing in his wings. Amen.

PART IV

How do I live as a disciple of Christ?

Lord, let me be obedient without arguing,
humble without feigning,
patient without grudging, pure without corruption,
merry without lightness, sad without mistrust,
sober without dullness, true without duplicity,
fearing you without desperation,
and trusting you without presumption.
Let me be joyful for nothing but that which pleases you,
and sorrowful for nothing but what displeases you:
that labor be my delight which is for you,
and let all weary me that is not in you.
Give me a waking spirit, and a diligent soul,
that I may seek to know your will,
and when I know it may I perform it faithfully
to the honor and glory of your ever blessed name.
Amen.

WEEK 40

Lord, let me be obedient without arguing, humble without feigning

SCRIPTURE

Then Moses went up to God; the LORD called to him from the mountain, saying, "Thus you shall say to the house of Jacob, and tell the Israelites: You have seen what I did to the Egyptians, and how I bore you on eagles' wings and brought you to myself. Now therefore, if you obey my voice and keep my covenant, you shall be my treasured possession out of all the peoples. Indeed, the whole earth is mine, but you shall be for me a priestly kingdom and a holy nation. These are the words that you shall speak to the Israelites." So Moses came, summoned the elders of the people, and set before them all these words that the LORD had commanded him. The people all answered as one: "Everything that the LORD has spoken we will do."—Exodus 19:3-8

MEDITATION

At the beginning of this final section of this life-shaping prayer, we return to the central theme of obedience. Obedience and humility go hand in hand because they reflect the attitudes and actions of a will turned either toward God or self. The great Protestant reformers were united in their diagnosis of the human predicament. A heart turned in upon itself obstructs the path to health and wholeness for the child of God.

The issue of obedience, of course, stretches back to the dawn of time. But this concern comes to a head within the community led by Moses through the wilderness journey. Despite the fact that Yahweh delivered the Israelites from captivity and bore them on eagles' wings, disobedience continued to plague their relationship. In our text for today, "the people all answered as one and said: 'All that the Lord has spoken we will do.'" But we know their resolve was short-lived. God had to call them back repeatedly. We delude ourselves if we think we are any different.

The sacrament of Holy Communion seals God's New Covenant. It reminds us of God's steadfast commitment to us and opens our hearts to God's transforming work. In a hymn describing the nature of sacrifice in the Sacrament, Charles Wesley turns to the issue of the will. Our desire to "pay thee all thy grace hath lent" comes not from a slavish fear of God's judgment but from a longing to please God through a will turned by God's grace to Jesus.

HYMN

This hymn can be sung to Sussex Carol, the tune used for "As Man and Woman We Were Made." Meter: 88.88.88

> Father, on us the Spirit bestow,
>> Through which thine everlasting Son
> Offered himself for us below,

That we, even we, before thy throne
Our souls and bodies may present,
  And pay thee all thy grace hath lent.

O let thy Spirit sanctify
  Whate'er to thee we now restore,
And make us with thy will comply;
  With all our mind, and soul, and power
Obey thee, as thy saints above,
In perfect innocence and love.

PRAYER

Gracious Lord, Creator and Redeemer, you are the author of being and life: inspire in me a spirit of praise and a desire to obey you in all things, that I may bring honor to your name in everything I think and say and do, through Jesus Christ my Lord. Amen.

WEEK 41

Patient without grudging, pure without corruption

SCRIPTURE

What sort of persons ought you to be in leading lives of holiness and godliness, waiting for and hastening the coming of the day of God . . . ? But, in accordance with his promise, we wait for new heavens and a new earth, where righteousness is at home. Therefore, beloved, while you are waiting for these things, strive to be found by him at peace, without spot or blemish. . . . But grow in the grace and knowledge of our Lord and Savior Jesus Christ. To him be the glory both now and to the day of eternity. Amen.—2 Peter 3:11-14, 18

MEDITATION

The writer of Second Peter admonishes his readers who await the return of Christ "to be found by him at peace, without spot or blemish." They wait with patience; they emulate the purity of their Lord. These followers of Jesus who lived in what they considered to be the end times poured all their energy into maintaining spotless lives. Their vision of an imminent end most certainly fueled this passion. Living each day as if it were their last provided the impetus to be and give their best to the highest glory of God.

Charles Wesley's concept of purity or spotlessness in terms of love for God and neighbor potentially safeguards a vision of perfection from the pathology of perfectionism. In the familiar hymn "Love Divine, All Loves Excelling" he prays for a love-filled life. Originally entitled "Thy Kingdom Come," perhaps no hymn has inspired more people to open their lives to the outpouring of God's love. Since Jesus is "pure, unbounded love," when his Spirit takes full possession of our souls, we reflect the "pure and spotless" image of God's new creation in him. Wesley acknowledges God as the source of a love that excels all others. God breathes the loving Spirit into every trembling heart when, in faith, we open our lives expectantly to Christ. Love liberates! It frees us to be the true children of the Lord of love. Pray to be lost in this wonder, love, and praise!

HYMN

This hymn can be sung to Hyfrydol, its traditional setting. Meter: 87.87 D

> Love divine, all loves excelling,
> > Joy of heaven, to earth come down,
> Fix in us thy humble dwelling,
> > All thy faithful mercies crown!
> Jesu, thou art all compassion,
> > Pure, unbounded love thou art;
> Visit us with thy salvation!
> > Enter every trembling heart.
>
> Finish then thy new creation,
> > Pure and spotless let us be;

Let us see thy great salvation
    Perfectly restored in thee;
Changed from glory into glory,
    Till in heaven we take our place,
Till we cast our crowns before thee,
    Lost in wonder, love, and praise.

PRAYER

Gracious Lord, pure and spotless Lamb of God by whom the whole world is redeemed: grant that I may become holy even as Jesus Christ is pure; that when he shall appear in power and glory, I may be made like him in his eternal and glorious reign. Amen.

WEEK 42

Merry without lightness, sad without mistrust

SCRIPTURE

When Jesus saw the crowds, he went up the mountain; and after he sat down, his disciples came to him. Then he began to speak, and taught them, saying: "Blessed are the poor in spirit, for theirs is the kingdom of heaven. Blessed are those who mourn, for they will be comforted. Blessed are the meek, for they will inherit the earth. Blessed are those who hunger and thirst for righteousness, for they will be filled. Blessed are the merciful, for they will receive mercy. Blessed are the pure in heart, for they will see God. Blessed are the peacemakers, for they will be called children of God. Blessed are those who are persecuted for righteousness' sake, for theirs is the kingdom of heaven."—Matthew 5:1-10

MEDITATION

In the New Testament, the word usually translated "blessed" can also be translated as "happy." For Methodists, holiness means happiness. *Blessed, holy, happy*—these words all mean the same thing. I think the prayer's author had this in mind when, in a somewhat enigmatic turn of phrase, he prayed to be "merry without lightness, sad without mistrust." We experience blessedness in a thoroughly grounded happiness. Jesus preached about this happy, holy, blessed life in the Beatitudes of his Sermon on the Mount. The pursuit of happiness for happiness' sake seldom secures it. But those who dedicate themselves to purity, peace, and righteousness; those who empathize with others, grieve, and suffer for the sake of Christ; those who seek humility and meekness discover true happiness through surrender to God's way.

The standard Jewish prayer begins with the words *Baruch Atah Adonai Eloheinu*, "Blessed are you, O Lord our God." In prayer and life we bless God; God grants true happiness to those who seek to live in conformity to God's will and way. It is interesting that Luke's version of the Beatitudes contrasts four blessings with four curses. Jesus declares blessing upon those who are poor and hated, those who hunger and weep. He warns of woe for those who are rich and popular, for those who have plenty to eat while others go hungry, for those who enjoy a good time while others suffer. The Beatitudes, like Wesley's hymn, point us back to the source of true happiness. With him we pray: "Set up thy kingdom (thy blessed rule) in my heart."

HYMN

This hymn can be sung to Saint Catherine, the tune used for "Faith of Our Fathers." Meter: 88.88.88

> Jesu, if still the same thou art,
> > If all thy promises are sure,
> Set up thy kingdom in my heart,
> > And make me rich, for I am poor:

To me be all thy treasures given,
    The kingdom of an inward heaven.

Where is the blessedness bestowed
    On all that hunger after thee?
I hunger now, I thirst for God!
See the poor fainting sinner, see,
    And satisfy with endless peace,
And fill me with thy righteousness.

Lord, I believe the promise sure,
    And trust thou wilt not long delay;
Hungry, and sorrowful, and poor,
    Upon thy word myself I stay;
Into thine hands my all resign,
And wait till all thou art is mine!

PRAYER

Gracious Lord, through Jesus, our eternal Spring, you have given us the water of life: make me thirst for him that I may turn aside from all lesser thirsts, through him who lives and reigns with you and the Holy Spirit, one God for ever and ever. Amen.

WEEK 43

Sober without dullness, true without duplicity

SCRIPTURE

So then let us not fall asleep as others do, but let us keep awake and be sober; for those who sleep sleep at night, and those who are drunk get drunk at night. But since we belong to the day, let us be sober, and put on the breastplate of faith and love, and for a helmet the hope of salvation. For God has destined us not for wrath but for obtaining salvation through our Lord Jesus Christ, who died for us, so that whether we are awake or asleep we may live with him.—1 Thessalonians 5:6-10

MEDITATION

Disciples of Christ must stay alert, guard the treasure of faith, and care for the gifts with which God arms them for the spiritual battles of life. In the sixth chapter of Ephesians, Christians are instructed to put on the whole armor of God. John Wesley published sixteen stanzas of his brother's poetic exposition of this text at the conclusion of his important treatise *The Character of a Methodist*. Stanzas from this frequently published hymn appeared in different configurations in several hymn collections because their spiritual wisdom was valued. Like the letter to the Ephesians, Wesley's hymn encouraged Christians to face and resist the forces of evil with courage.

According to the scripture passage for today, those who

are sober and align themselves with truth put on the breast-plate of faith and love. The hope of salvation guards their minds like a helmet. God strengthens people in overcoming temptation to deviate from the path Christ sets before us when the battles of life rage. When feeling weak and unequal to the task, the Christian disciple trusts in the strength of Jesus. To walk with Christ requires vigilance in prayer. The children of God keep their eyes open, exercise their gifts, and use every grace that God supplies to embrace Jesus' reign. The arduous journey of discipleship requires all of these activities and practices. "Take every virtue, every grace," sings Wesley, "arm yourselves with all the mind that was in Christ your head."

HYMN

This hymn can be sung to Diademata, the traditional setting for this hymn. Meter: SMD

> Soldiers of Christ, arise,
> And put your armor on,
> Strong in the strength which God supplies
> Through his eternal Son;
> Strong in the Lord of hosts,
> And in his mighty power,
> Who in the strength of Jesus trusts
> Is more than conqueror.
>
> To keep your armor bright
> Attend with constant care;
> Still walking in your Captain's sight,
> And watching unto prayer;
> Ready for all alarms,
> Steadfastly set your face,

And always exercise your arms,
    And use your every grace.

Leave no unguarded place,
    No weakness of the soul;
Take every virtue, every grace,
    And fortify the whole;
    Indissolubly joined,
    To battle all proceed,
But arm yourselves with all the mind
    That was in Christ your head.

PRAYER

Gracious Lord, whose Son Jesus Christ is the way, the truth, and the life: teach me to walk in his way, to rejoice in his truth, to share in his risen life, and to arm myself with all the mind that was in him, who lives and reigns with you and the Holy Spirit forever. Amen.

WEEK 44

*Fearing you without desperation,
and trusting you without presumption*

SCRIPTURE

O Israel, trust in the LORD!
　　　He is their help and their shield.
O house of Aaron, trust in the LORD!
　　　He is their help and their shield.
You who fear the LORD, trust in the LORD!
　　　He is their help and their shield.

The LORD has been mindful of us; he will bless us;
　　　he will bless the house of Israel;
　　　he will bless the house of Aaron;
he will bless those who fear the LORD,
　　　both small and great.

　　　. . . . .

But we will bless the LORD
　　　from this time on and forevermore.
Praise the LORD!—Psalm 115:9-13, 18

MEDITATION

"[God] is their help and their shield." This portion of Psalm 115 returns to central themes in David's songs: the fear of the Lord, trust in the Lord, and God as shield and defender. Given the repetition of these themes throughout the scriptures, and in the Psalms in particular, God's people need to hear these words of comfort time and time again. They reflect the sentiment of Elizabeth's prayer to fear God without desperation and trust God without presumption.

In 1759, following the English capture of Quebec during the French and Indian Wars, Charles Wesley published a series of *Thanksgiving Hymns* to celebrate the British victory in the new world. In the first stanza of the following hymn, he reminds us that God is still in control. Despite all appearances, despite the gathering clouds and mounting storm, the Lord rescues those who put their trust in God. Whenever we experience God's shield of protection, ecstasy displaces the anxiety and gloom that threaten to steal our joy in life.

The second stanza affirms total dependence on Christ alone. Our ultimate salvation rests in God and in God alone. The One who redeems us in Christ will save us to the end if we put our trust and confidence in him. We rest in his name. We trust in his nature.

The final stanza describes the One in whom we place our trust, the shield who protects. Truth, wisdom, power, justice, and grace in the Savior elicit our adoration and praise. His name is Jesus and his nature is pure, universal love for all.

HYMN

This hymn can be sung to Hanover, the tune used for "Ye Servants of God." Meter: 10.10.11.11

Give glory to God who sits on the throne,
And scatters the proud, And rescues his own!
Our best adoration To him we will give,
And all his salvation With rapture receive.

Our safety on him Alone doth depend:
Who now doth redeem Shall save to the end:
Almighty Creator, We rest in thy name,
We trust in thy nature, For ever the same.

Thy name we adore, Thine attributes praise,
Truth, wisdom, and power, And justice and grace!
To ransom and bless us, Thou cam'st from above;
Thy name it is Jesus, Thy nature is love.

PRAYER

Gracious Lord, God of light and glory, you are the beauty I seek and the power to whom I entrust my life: enable me to rest in the knowledge of your love and care so that through the witness of my life, others might come to know you as you truly are. Amen.

WEEK 45

Let me be joyful for nothing but that which pleases you

SCRIPTURE

Do not be deceived; God is not mocked, for you reap whatever you sow. If you sow to your own flesh, you will reap corruption from the flesh; but if you sow to the Spirit, you will reap eternal life from the Spirit. So let us not grow weary in doing what is right, for we will reap at harvest time, if we do not give up. So then, whenever we have an opportunity, let us work for the good of all, and especially for those of the family of faith.—Galatians 6:7-10

MEDITATION

"Do good." John Wesley drew up "General Rules" to govern the life of the Methodist movement. Their simplicity is startling—only three rules: Avoid evil. Do good. Immerse yourself in the means of grace. The Wesleys never abandoned the foundation of faith for salvation but also realized that everyday actions reflect the character of those who claim to be Christ's. Disciples seek to please God by practicing goodness.

Charles Wesley's hymn, originally titled "Before Work," reflects a Christian attitude about the dailiness of discipleship and the presence of God in the common tasks of life. He composed his hymn in the spirit of Paul: "let us work for the good of all." Wesley lays down four clear principles related to our good work in the world. First, we resolve to know God in all our daily activities. We seek to reflect God's goodness in all we think, speak, and do. Second, we approach our appointed work with cheerfulness, knowing that a greater wisdom lies behind all circumstances in life. We can find God in everything; every moment becomes an opportunity to celebrate God's presence. Third, we intentionally offer a place of honor to God in our work and welcome Christ as our companion. Those who are yoked to Goodness itself discover the sheer joy of doing good. Fourth, we use our gifts, graciously bestowed by God, for the good of all. "Even joy" characterizes those who choose this course in life.

HYMN

This hymn can be sung to Duke Street, its traditional setting.
Meter: LM

Forth in thy name, O Lord, I go,
  My daily labor to pursue,
Thee, only thee, resolved to know
  In all I think, or speak, or do.

The task thy wisdom has assigned
  O let me cheerfully fulfil,
In all my works thy presence find,
  And prove thy good and perfect will.

Thee may I set at my right hand
    Whose eyes my inmost substance see,
And labor on at thy command,
    And offer all my works to thee.

For thee delightfully employ
    Whate'er thy bounteous grace hath given,
And run my course with even joy,
    And closely walk with thee to heaven.

PRAYER

Gracious Lord, in my weakness I can do nothing good without you, but you supply to me all you demand of me through your grace: grant me such grace to keep your commandments that I may please you both in will and in deed, through Jesus Christ my Lord. Amen.

WEEK 46

And sorrowful for nothing but what displeases you

SCRIPTURE

Depart from evil, and do good;
> so you shall abide forever.
For the Lord loves justice;
> he will not forsake his faithful ones.
The righteous shall be kept safe forever,
> but the children of the wicked shall be cut off.
The righteous shall inherit the land,
> and live in it forever.

The mouths of the righteous utter wisdom,
> and their tongues speak justice.
The law of their God is in their hearts;
> their steps do not slip.

. . . .

Mark the blameless, and behold the upright,
> for there is posterity for the peaceable.

—Psalm 37:27-31, 37

MEDITATION

God not only shapes our lives by what we do proactively but by what we avoid. John Wesley's second General Rule is "Avoid evil." Psalm 37 makes it clear that doing good and avoiding evil go hand in hand. Both are active practices. Living in God's reign means aligning oneself with the quest for justice and peace. But it also entails resisting evil so that God can open a space for us to embrace justice and love.

No greater evil dominates the landscape of human history than war. Charles Wesley wrote few antiwar poems, but several of his hymns shatter any romantic illusions about war and illuminate its true nature as the sum of all evils. The larger context of one diatribe against war is prayer for humankind, published among his *Intercession Hymns* in 1758. Wesley's graphic imagery shocks the singer out of complacency: violence, wrong, and cruelty pervade God's good earth. Wesley depicts God's creatures as enemies who tear each other apart "in all the hellish rage of war." They turn God's glorious creation into "one wide-extended field of blood."

The closing stanzas appeal to all that is good and true in the human creature. Avoiding this great evil and following the path to shalom rest on the same principles. Discord is "unnatural." Reconciliation is God's way. Acts of kindness constitute the transformed heart. Jesus' disciples are committed to God's righteous reign, "The paradise of perfect love!" Perhaps no greater challenge confronts us in our own time: avoid evil, resist war, pray for peace.

HYMN

This hymn can be sung to Selena, the tune used for "O Love Divine, What Hast Thou Done." Meter: 88.88.88

Our earth we now lament to see
    With floods of wickedness o'erflowed:
With violence, wrong, and cruelty,
    One wide-extended field of blood,
Where men, like fiends each other tear,
In all the hellish rage of war.

O might the universal Friend
    This havoc of his creatures see!
Bid our unnatural discord end;
    Declare us reconciled in thee!
Write kindness on our inward parts
And chase the murderer from our hearts!

Who now against each other rise,
    The nations of the earth constrain
To follow after peace, and prize
    The blessings of thy righteous reign,
The joys of unity to prove,
The paradise of perfect love!

PRAYER

Gracious Lord, God of glory and of might, you created the world in power and redeemed it in love: grant me the grace to live the good news of your reign in justice and truth, in mercy and peace, that others may come to believe in Jesus Christ, my risen Lord and Savior. Amen.

WEEK 47

That labor be my delight which is for you

SCRIPTURE

So now, O Israel, what does the LORD your God require of you? Only to fear the LORD your God, to walk in all his ways, to love him, to serve the LORD your God with all your heart and with all your soul, and to keep the commandments of the LORD your God and his decrees that I am commanding you today, for your own well-being. Although heaven and the heaven of heavens belong to the LORD your God, the earth with all that is in it, yet the LORD set his heart in love on your ancestors alone and chose you, their descendants after them, out of all the peoples, as it is today. . . . You shall fear the LORD your God; him alone you shall worship; to him you shall hold fast, and by his name you shall swear. He is your praise; he is your God, who has done for you these great and awesome things that your own eyes have seen.— Deuteronomy 10:12-15, 20-21

MEDITATION

Discipleship in the Methodist tradition consists in serving God with a willing and joyful heart. God calls us to this service. The Holy Spirit empowers us to fulfill our calling. Conformity to the mind of Christ fills us with a peace that passes all understanding. The motto "believe, love, serve" epitomizes the Wesley family. These three words sum up the abundant life of a child of God. Only those know its joy who have been liberated to become their true selves as transcripts of God's "infinite love."

The background to Charles Wesley's familiar hymn "Ye Servants of God" elucidates this servant discipleship more fully. Wesley included this summons to servanthood among his *Hymns for Times of Trouble and Persecution*, published in 1744 in the middle of a tumultuous decade for the early Methodists. Political upheaval divided England, and some of the Wesleys' detractors wrongfully claimed they were disloyal to the king, supporting a pretender to the throne. In the midst of this struggle related to the monarchy, Charles left no doubt about his loyalty to the king, but he also grasped the opportunity to demonstrate the ultimate allegiance of the Methodists to God. Only the kingdom of this eternal Sovereign is truly glorious. It is only appropriate to ascribe all glory and power, wisdom and might, honor and blessing to this Monarch who rules over all! We serve earthly rulers, to be sure, but Jesus calls us to serve God and honor God's rule above all others.

HYMN

This hymn can be sung to Hanover, its traditional setting. Meter: 10.10.11.11

> Ye servants of God, Your Master proclaim,
> And publish abroad His wonderful name;

The name all-victorious Of Jesus extol,
His kingdom is glorious, And rules over all.

God ruleth on high, Almighty to save,
And still he is nigh, His presence we have;
The great congregation His triumph shall sing,
Ascribing salvation To Jesus, our King.

Then let us adore, And give him his right,
All glory and power, All wisdom and might;
All honor and blessing With angels above,
And thanks never ceasing And infinite love.

PRAYER

Gracious Lord, by whose grace alone I have been accepted and called to your service: strengthen me by your Holy Spirit and make me truly worthy of my calling to proclaim Jesus through the witness of my life, to the glory of his ever blessed name. Amen.

WEEK 48

And let all weary me that is not in you

SCRIPTURE

Have you not known? Have you not heard?
The LORD is the everlasting God,
    the Creator of the ends of the earth.
He does not faint or grow weary;
    his understanding is unsearchable.
He gives power to the faint,
    and strengthens the powerless.
Even youths will faint and be weary,
    and the young will fall exhausted;
but those who wait for the LORD shall renew their strength,
    they shall mount up with wings like eagles,
they shall run and not be weary,
    they shall walk and not faint.—Isaiah 40:28-31

MEDITATION

For the mature disciple of Christ, those things that are not godly weary the soul, but engagement in those actions that reflect God's will and way elevate the spirit. When we view our sinful actions for what they actually are—rebellion against God—they burden us. We long to rid ourselves of all the weight that slows us to the goal.

When I taught at Africa University in Zimbabwe, one of my students was a young woman preparing for the ministry. She told me she didn't think God intended Christians simply to struggle through their days. God didn't create us just to muddle through. She wanted to fly, to soar through life. Her statement reminded me of the stanza in Charles Wesley's great resurrection hymn, "Christ the Lord Is Risen Today."

Soar we now where Christ has led,
　　　Following our exalted Head,
Made like him, like him we rise,
　　　Ours the cross, the grave, the skies.

Christ has won the victory over death and the grave. Our joys and triumphs rise to heights unknown. In Christ, we soar! The prophet Isaiah participated in this resurrection vision long before the time of Jesus. He knew something about the power of God to elevate those created in the very image of God. "They shall mount up with wings like eagles, they shall run and not be weary, they shall walk and not faint." Rise up, O child of God.

HYMN

This hymn can be sung to Easter Hymn, its traditional setting. Meter: 77.77 D

"Christ the Lord is risen today," [Alleluia!]
Earth and heaven in chorus say, [Alleluia!]
Raise your joys and triumphs high, [Alleluia!]
Sing, ye heavens, and earth reply. [Alleluia!]

Love's redeeming work is done; [Alleluia!]
    Fought the fight, the battle won, [Alleluia!]
Death in vain forbids him rise, [Alleluia!]
    Christ has opened paradise, [Alleluia!]

Lives again our glorious King, [Alleluia!]
    Where, O death, is now thy sting? [Alleluia!]
Once he died our souls to save, [Alleluia!]
    Where's thy victory, boasting grave? [Alleluia!]

Soar we now where Christ has led, [Alleluia!]
    Following our exalted Head, [Alleluia!]
Made like him, like him we rise, [Alleluia!]
    Ours the cross, the grave, the skies. [Alleluia!]

PRAYER

Gracious Lord, who brought your beloved Son from the dead and in your great mercy made the disciples glad with the sight of the risen Lord: through the Spirit's gift of faith, enable us to soar where Christ had led; make us, like him, to rise in newness of life. Amen.

WEEK 49

Give me a waking spirit, and a diligent soul

SCRIPTURE

Beware, keep alert; for you do not know when the time will come. It is like a man going on a journey, when he leaves home and puts his slaves in charge, each with his work, and commands the doorkeeper to be on the watch. Therefore, keep awake—for you do not know when the master of the house will come, in the evening, or at midnight, or at cock-crow, or at dawn, or else he may find you asleep when he comes suddenly. And what I say to you I say to all: Keep awake.—Mark 13:33-37

MEDITATION

As we come close to the end of our journey, we return to the theme of watchfulness. "Beware, keep alert," the Markan evangelist exclaims. "Keep awake." God trusts us enough to put demanding work into our hands, particularly the hard work of love that requires constant vigilance.

In "A Charge to Keep I Have," Charles Wesley reflects upon an incident recorded in Leviticus 8:35: "You shall remain at the entrance of the tent of meeting . . . , keeping the Lord's charge so that you do not die." This sixteen-line hymn teaches us much about the life of discipleship. First, we all receive a charge from God that is timely and engages us fully. When I taught at the new Asbury Theological Seminary campus in Orlando, Florida, I was impressed at the first commencement when the president gave a charge to the graduating class. All the graduates were commissioned to practice the way of Jesus in their ministry, but each was called to live out that commission according to his or her unique identity. Wesley charges us to glorify God, but each person must discern a singular way to honor God with the gift of her or his life.

Second, we live out our charge in the presence of God and through the practice of prayer. We are accountable to the God who knows and loves us completely. Attentiveness to God in prayer deepens the bond of faith, hope, and love with the One who has created us to serve the present age. When we rely on God, God supplies what God demands.

HYMN

This hymn can be sung to Boylston, its traditional setting. Meter: SM

> A charge to keep I have,
> A God to glorify,
> A never-dying soul to save,
> And fit it for the sky;
> To serve the present age,
> My calling to fulfil;
> O may it all my powers engage
> To do my Master's will!

Arm me with jealous care,
As in thy sight to live;
And Oh! thy servant, Lord, prepare
A strict account to give.
Help me to watch and pray,
And on thyself rely,
Assured, if I my trust betray,
I shall for ever die.

PRAYER

Gracious Lord, you spoke through the prophets that they might make your will and purpose known: help me to watch and pray so as never to forget that my calling is to serve in the world, to seek the lost whom you love, and to glorify you in all that I do for Jesus' sake. Amen.

WEEK 50

That I may seek to know your will

SCRIPTURE

One of the scribes came near and heard them disputing with one another, and seeing that he answered them well, he asked him, "Which commandment is the first of all?" Jesus answered, "The first is, 'Hear, O Israel: the Lord our God, the Lord is one; you shall love the Lord your God with all your heart, and with all your soul, and with all your mind, and with all your strength.' The second is this, 'You shall love your neighbor as yourself.' There is no other commandment greater than these." Then the scribe said to him, "You are right, Teacher; you have truly said that 'he is one, and besides him there is no other'; and 'to love him with all the heart, and with all the understanding, and with all the strength,' and 'to love one's neighbor as oneself,'—this is much more important than all whole burnt offerings and sacrifices." When Jesus saw that he answered wisely, he said to him, "You are not far from the kingdom of God."—Mark 12:28-34

MEDITATION

What is God's will? A scribe posed this question to Jesus in a slightly different form: "Which commandment is the first of all?" Jesus answered unequivocally: "Love God with your whole being; love your neighbor as yourself." Seeking to know the will of God brings us all close to God's reign—God's purpose for creation and our place within it. When asked about the purpose of religion or the goal of life in Christ, John Wesley articulated his response in the same way—love God, love others. He defined holiness as love. It is not surprising that this ultimate question figures prominently at the close of the prayer Elizabeth committed to memory. To know God's will means to practice love for God and love for others.

In our hymn today, Charles Wesley reflects upon the will of God we seek to know. The four stanzas illuminate the central affirmations of the Methodist way. First, God wills for you to be holy. Conformity to God's will is measured by your degree of love to God and neighbor. Second, immersion in God's love is the path to holiness. "Plunge me, every whit made whole," Wesley prays, "In all the depths of love divine!" Third, God sustains your journey when you root your life in God's promises. You can depend upon the Spirit to fulfill God's will for you. Fourth, God will restore love to your soul if you pray for it earnestly. "Come, Savior, come, and make me whole!"

HYMN

This hymn can be sung to Rockingham, the tune for "When I Survey the Wondrous Cross." Meter: 88.88

> He wills that I should holy be;
>> That holiness I long to feel,

That full divine conformity
    To all my Savior's righteous will.

See, Lord, the travail of thy soul
    Accomplished in the change of mine;
And plunge me, every whit made whole,
    In all the depths of love divine!

On thee, O God, my soul is stayed,
    And waits to prove thine utmost will;
The promise, by thy mercy made,
    Thou canst, thou wilt in me fulfil.

Come, Savior, come, and make me whole!
    Entirely all my sins remove;
To perfect health restore my soul,
    To perfect holiness and love.

PRAYER

Gracious Lord, holy and life-giving God, your will is that I be made whole through the healing of your Son: grant me the grace to love you with my whole heart, soul, mind, and strength and to love my neighbor as myself, for in this perfect holiness is my greatest happiness in life. Amen.

WEEK 51

And when I know it may I perform it faithfully

SCRIPTURE

What good is it, my brothers and sisters, if you say you have faith but do not have works? Can faith save you? If a brother or sister is naked and lacks daily food, and one of you says to them, "Go in peace; keep warm and eat your fill," and yet you do not supply their bodily needs, what is the good of that? So faith by itself, if it has no works, is dead. But someone will say, "You have faith and I have works." Show me your faith apart from your works, and I by my works will show you my faith. . . . For just as the body without the spirit is dead, so faith without works is also dead.—James 2:14-18, 26

MEDITATION

To know the will of God is one thing; to do it is something else altogether. The prayer to know God's will finds an essential counterpart in the petition, "And when I know it may I perform it faithfully." The movement from knowing to doing eludes many. Some Christians, in fact, seem to fixate upon knowing God, while others care only about action. The

Methodist way holds both together, the knowing and the doing, the creed and the deed, faith and works.

The author of James demonstrates the integral nature of faith and works. "Show me your faith apart from your works," we read, "and I by my works will show you my faith." One of the most profound explications of this dynamic conjunction is Wesley's poetic exposition of Ephesians 2:8-10. He captures the essence of fulfilling God's will in the final line of the hymn: "Saved by faith which works by love." The hymn opens with a strong appeal to "faith alone," the watch cry of the Protestant reformers, but this faith is active. God justifies, according to Wesley, but works demonstrate God's gift of faith. God wills for the Spirit to shape the Savior in the soul of every person. This life-transforming experience forms character, attitude, and behavior in the faithful disciple. God also wills for all to experience the heaven of love here on earth. To do the will of God means to accept the gift of faith and to grow into the loving image of Christ.

HYMN

This hymn can be sung to Savannah, its traditional setting. Meter: 77.77

> Plead we thus for faith alone,
> Faith which by our works is shown;
> God it is who justifies,
> Only faith the grace applies,
> Active faith that lives within,
> Conquers earth, and hell, and sin,
> Sanctifies, and makes us whole,
> Forms the Savior in the soul.

Let us for this faith contend,
Sure salvation is its end;
Heaven already is begun,
Everlasting life is won.
Only let us persevere
Till we see our Lord appear;
Never from the rock remove,
Saved by faith which works by love.

PRAYER

Gracious Lord, almighty and ever-living God, increase your gift of faith in me, that, forsaking all that lies behind, I might reach out toward the fullest possible love and run the way of your commandments, saved by faith made effective through love, for Christ's sake. Amen.

WEEK 52

To the honor and glory of your ever blessed name. Amen

SCRIPTURE

The God who made the world and everything in it, he who is Lord of heaven and earth, does not live in shrines made by human hands, nor is he served by human hands, as though he needed anything, since he himself gives to all mortals life and breath and all things. From one ancestor he made all nations to inhabit the whole earth, and he allotted the times of their existence and the boundaries of the places where they would live, so that they would search for God and perhaps grope for him and find him—though indeed he is not far from each one of us. For "In him we live and move and have our being."—Acts 17:24-28

MEDITATION

Through prayer we worship God. In a life of prayer we offer up every thought, word, and deed "to the honor and glory of God's ever blessed name" because "in [God] we live and move and have our being." Worship can be defined in many ways, but every understanding of worship involves reciprocal action. God reveals God's self to us, and we offer ourselves to God in response. We remember God's mighty acts of salvation in order to be drawn into the amazing story of God's love. In worship, the Spirit descends upon us anew to lift us into the presence of the blessed Trinity.

Charles Wesley's lyrical reflection upon Acts 17:28 provides a fitting conclusion to our journey. In this final meditation, we offer a doxology of praise to God the Maker, the Incarnate Deity, and the Sacred Spirit. We proclaim honor and glory to God's blessed name first and foremost because of God's creating love. Everything begins and ends in this love, and the joyful song of love echoes to the skies. This love came down at Christmas. In Jesus Christ, God became flesh and dwelt among us, full of grace and truth. We encounter the one, true God in Jesus, and we experience God's redeeming love. The Holy Spirit, Wesley maintains, is a Spirit of holiness, a sacred energy that renews the hearts of God's children in every age. Through the Spirit, God manifests the unspeakable love at the core of the Trinity, a relational love that restores all things and makes us whole. Dwell upon this love!

HYMN

This hymn can be sung to Diademata, its traditional setting. Meter: SMD

> Maker, in whom we live,
> > In whom we are and move
> The glory, power, and praise receive
> > For thy creating love.
> Let all the angel throng
> > Give thanks to God on high,
> While earth repeats the joyful song
> > And echoes to the sky.

Incarnate Deity,
    Let all the ransomed race
Render in thanks their lives to thee
    For thy redeeming grace.
The grace to sinners showed
    Ye heavenly choirs proclaim,
And cry, "Salvation to our God,
    Salvation to the Lamb!"

Spirit of holiness,
    Let all thy saints adore
Thy sacred energy, and bless
    Thine heart-renewing power.
Not angel tongues can tell
    Thy love's ecstatic height,
The glorious joy unspeakable,
    The beatific sight.

Eternal, Triune God,
    Let all the hosts above,
Let all on earth below record
    And dwell upon thy love.
When heaven and earth are fled
    Before thy glorious face,
Sing all the saints thy love hath made
    Thine everlasting praise.

PRAYER

Gracious Lord, you have given me grace to acknowledge the glory of the eternal Three-One God: keep me steadfast in this faith and worship, and bring me at last to dwell upon your love throughout all eternity, to the honor and glory of your ever blessed name. Amen.

A COLLECT TEMPLATE

1. An address to God
   (Almighty God,)
2. A reference to some divine attribute or act as a ground for prayer
   (to you all hearts are open, all desires known, and from you no secrets are hidden:)
3. The prayer proper—short, simple, and definite
   (Cleanse the thoughts of our hearts by the inspiration of your Holy Spirit, that we may perfectly love you, and worthily magnify your holy name;)
4. A concluding doxology
   (through Christ our Lord. Amen.)

OTHER SAMPLE COLLECTS
FROM THE BOOK OF COMMON PRAYER

O God, the author of peace and lover of concord, to know you is eternal life and to serve you is perfect freedom: Defend us, your humble servants, in all assaults of our enemies; that we, surely trusting in your defense, may not fear the power of any adversaries; through the might of Jesus Christ our Lord. Amen.

Lord Jesus Christ, you stretched out your arms of love on the hard wood of the cross that everyone might come within the reach of your saving embrace: So clothe us in your Spirit that we, reaching forth our hands in love, may bring those who do not know you to the knowledge and love of you; for the honor of your Name. Amen.

MORNING PRAYER
FROM THE BOOK OF COMMON PRAYER

CALL TO PRAYER
>Lord, open our lips.
>>**And our mouth shall proclaim your praise.**

Glory to the Father, and to the Son, and to the Holy Spirit: as it was in the beginning, is now, and will be for ever. Amen. Alleluia.

PSALM 95:1-7

>O come, let us sing to the Lord;
>>let us make a joyful noise to the
>>>rock of our salvation!
>Let us come into his presence with
>>thanksgiving;
>>let us make a joyful noise to
>him with songs of praise!
>For the LORD is a great God,
>>and a great King above all gods.
>In his hand are the depths of the earth;
>the heights of the mountains are his also.
>The sea is his, for he made it,
>>and the dry land, which his
>hands have formed.

O come, let us worship and bow down,
    let us kneel before the LORD, our Maker!
For he is our God,
    and we are the people of his pasture,
and the sheep of his hand.

O that today you would listen to his voice!

Glory to the Father, and to the Son, and to the Holy Spirit:
as it was in the beginning, is now, and will be for ever.
Amen. Alleluia.

SCRIPTURE READING FOR THE DAY

TIME OF REFLECTION

THE TE DEUM

You are God: we praise you;
You are the Lord: we acclaim you;
You are the eternal Father:
All creation worships you.
To you all angels, all the powers of heaven,
Cherubim and Seraphim, sing in endless praise:
    Holy, holy, holy Lord, God of power and might,
    heaven and earth are full of your glory.
The glorious company of apostles praise you.
The noble fellowship of prophets praise you.
The white-robed army of martyrs praise you.
Throughout the world the holy Church acclaims you;
    Father, of majesty unbounded,
    your true and only Son, worthy of all worship,
    and the Holy Spirit, advocate and guide.

You, Christ, are the king of glory,
the eternal Son of the Father.
When you became man to set us free
you did not shun the Virgin's womb.
You overcame the sting of death
and opened the kingdom of heaven to all believers.
You are seated at God's right hand in glory.
We believe that you will come and be our judge.
    Come then, Lord, and help your people,
    bought with the price of your own blood,
    and bring us with your saints
    to glory everlasting.

THE MEDITATION FOR THE DAY

TIME OF REFLECTION

THE APOSTLES' CREED

I believe in God, the Father almighty,
    creator of heaven and earth.
I believe in Jesus Christ, his only Son, our Lord.
    He was conceived by the power of the Holy Spirit
    and born of the Virgin Mary.
    He suffered under Pontius Pilate,
    was crucified, died, and was buried.
    He descended to the dead.
    On the third day he rose again.
    He ascended into heaven,
    and is seated at the right hand of the Father.
    He will come again to judge the living and the dead.
I believe in the Holy Spirit,

the holy catholic Church,
the communion of saints,
the forgiveness of sins,
the resurrection of the body,
and the life everlasting. Amen.

THE HYMN FOR THE DAY

TIME OF REFLECTION

PRAYER

The Lord be with you.
And also with you.

Lord, have mercy upon us.
Christ, have mercy upon us.
Lord, have mercy upon us.

THE PRAYER FOR THE DAY

THE LORD'S PRAYER (traditional version)

Our Father, who art in heaven,
hallowed be thy Name.
thy kingdom come,
thy will be done,
on earth as it is in heaven.
Give us this day our daily bread.
And forgive us our trespasses,
as we forgive those
who trespass against us.
And lead us not into temptation,
but deliver us from evil.

For thine is the kingdom,
>> and the power, and the glory,
>> for ever and ever. Amen.

THE MORNING COLLECTS

Lord God, almighty and everlasting Father, you have brought us in safety to this new day: Preserve us with your mighty power, that we may not fall into sin, nor be overcome by adversity; and in all we do, direct us to the fulfilling of your purpose; through Jesus Christ our Lord. Amen.

Almighty God, you have given us grace at this time with one accord to make our common supplication to you; and you have promised through your well-beloved Son that when two or three are gathered together in his Name you will be in the midst of them: Fulfil now, O Lord, our desires and petitions as may be best for us; granting us in this world knowledge of your truth, and in the age to come life everlasting. Amen.

The grace of our Lord Jesus Christ, and the love of God, and the fellowship of the Holy Spirit, be with us all evermore. Amen.

EVENING PRAYER
FROM THE BOOK OF COMMON PRAYER

CALL TO PRAYER
O God, make speed to save us.
O Lord, make haste to help us.

Glory to the Father, and to the Son, and to the Holy Spirit: as it was in the beginning, is now, and will be for ever. Amen. Alleluia.

PSALM 98
O sing to the LORD a new song,
for he has done marvelous things.
His right hand and his holy arm
have gotten him victory.
The LORD has made known his victory;
he has revealed his vindication in the sight of
the nations.
He has remembered his steadfast love and
faithfulness
to the house of Israel.
All the ends of the earth have seen
the victory of our God.

Make a joyful noise to the LORD, all the earth;
break forth into joyous song and sing praises.

Sing praises to the Lord with the lyre,
>with the lyre and the sound of melody.
With trumpets and the sound of the horn
>make a joyful noise before the King, the Lord.

Let the sea roar, and all that fills it;
>the world and those who live in it.
Let the floods clap their hands;
>let the hills sing together for joy
at the presence of the Lord, for he is coming
>to judge the earth.
He will judge the world with righteousness,
>and the peoples with equity.

Glory to the Father, and to the Son, and to the Holy Spirit: as it was in the beginning, is now, and will be for ever. Amen. Alleluia.

SCRIPTURE READING FOR THE DAY

TIME OF REFLECTION

THE MAGNIFICAT

>**My soul magnifies the Lord,**
>>**and my spirit rejoices in God my Savior,**
>>**for he has looked with favor**
>>**on the lowliness of his servant.**
>**Surely, from now on all generations will call me blessed;**
>>**for the Mighty One has done great**
>>**things for me,**
>>**and holy is his name.**
>>**His mercy is for those who fear him**
>>**from generation to generation.**

He has shown strength with his arm;
>he has scattered the proud in the thoughts of
>>their hearts.
>He has brought down the powerful from their
>>thrones,
>and lifted up the lowly;
>>he has filled the hungry with good things,
>>and sent the rich away empty.
>He has helped his servant Israel,
>>in remembrance of his mercy,
>>according to the promise he made to our
>>>ancestors,
>>to Abraham and to his descendants forever.

THE MEDITATION FOR THE DAY

TIME OF REFLECTION

THE APOSTLES' CREED

I believe in God, the Father almighty,
>creator of heaven and earth.
I believe in Jesus Christ, his only Son, our Lord.
>He was conceived by the power of the Holy Spirit
>>and born of the Virgin Mary.
>He suffered under Pontius Pilate,
>>was crucified, died, and was buried.
>He descended to the dead.
>On the third day he rose again.
>He ascended into heaven,
>>and is seated at the right hand of the Father.
>He will come again to judge the living and the dead.
I believe in the Holy Spirit,

the holy catholic Church,
the communion of saints,
the forgiveness of sins,
the resurrection of the body,
and the life everlasting. Amen.

THE SONG OF SIMEON (Nunc dimittis)

Lord, you now have set your servant free
to go in peace as you have promised;
For these eyes of mine have seen the Savior,
whom you have prepared for all the world to see:
A Light to enlighten the nations,
and the glory of your people Israel.

Glory to the Father, and to the Son, and to the Holy Spirit: as it was in the beginning, is now, and will be for ever. Amen. Alleluia.

THE HYMN FOR THE DAY

TIME OF REFLECTION

PRAYER

The Lord be with you.
And also with you.

Lord, have mercy upon us.
Christ, have mercy upon us.
Lord, have mercy upon us.

THE PRAYER FOR THE DAY

THE LORD'S PRAYER (traditional version)

Our Father, who art in heaven,
hallowed be thy Name,
thy kingdom come,
thy will be done,
on earth as it is in heaven.
Give us this day our daily bread.
And forgive us our trespasses,
as we forgive those
who trespass against us.
And lead us not into temptation,
but deliver us from evil.
For thine is the kingdom,
and the power, and the glory,
for ever and ever. Amen.

THE EVENING COLLECTS (traditional versions)

Most holy God, the source of all good desires, all right judgments, and all just works: Give to us, your servants, that peace which the world cannot give, so that our minds may be fixed on the doing of your will, and that we, being delivered from the fear of all enemies, may live in peace and quietness; through the mercies of Christ Jesus our Savior. Amen.

Almighty God, you have given us grace at this time with one accord to make our common supplication to you; and you have promised through your well-beloved Son that when two or three are gathered together in his Name you will be in the midst of them: Fulfil now, O Lord, our desires and petitions as may be best for us;

granting us in this world knowledge of your truth, and
in the age to come life everlasting. Amen.

The grace of our Lord Jesus Christ, and the love of God, and the
fellowship of the Holy Spirit, be with us all evermore. Amen.

HYMN SOURCES
SHORT TITLES AND ABBREVIATIONS

Poetry/Hymn Publications by John and/or Charles Wesley

CPH (1738)	*A Collection of Psalms and Hymns* (London: [Bowyer], 1738)
CPH (1743)	*A Collection of Psalms and Hymns*, 2nd ed., enlarged (London: Strahan, 1743)
Family Hymns	*Hymns for the Use of Families, and on various Occasions* (Bristol: Pine, 1767)
HLS	*Hymns on the Lord's Supper* (Bristol: Farley, 1745)
HSP (1739)	*Hymns and Sacred Poems* (London: Strahan, 1739)
HSP (1740)	*Hymns and Sacred Poems* (London: Strahan, 1740)
HSP (1742)	*Hymns and Sacred Poems* (London: Farley, 1742)
HSP (1749)	*Hymns and Sacred Poems*, 2 vols. (Bristol, Farley, 1749)
HTTP	*Hymns for Times of Trouble and Persecution* (London: [Strahan], 1744)

Hymns (1780)	*A Collection of Hymns for the use of the People Called Methodists* (London: Paramore, 1780)
Hymns for Children	*Hymns for Children* (Bristol: Farley, 1763)
Intercession Hymns (1758)	*Hymns of Intercession for all Mankind* (Bristol: Farley, 1758)
Redemption Hymns	*Hymns for those that see, and those that have Redemption in the Blood of Jesus Christ* (London: Strahan, 1747)
Scripture Hymns	*Short Hymns on Select Passages of the Holy Scriptures*, 2 vols. (Bristol: Farley, 1762)
Thanksgiving Hymns (1759)	*Hymns to be Used on the Thanksgiving Day, Nov. 29, 1759* (London: Strahan, 1759)

HYMN SOURCE INDEX

Week	Hymn

1   *Hymns for Children*, Hymn 1.1, 6, 8; *Hymns* (1780), Hymn 229:1, 6, 8

2   *HSP* (1749), v. 1, pp. 251–52; *Hymns* (1780), Hymn 314:1-2

3   *HSP* (1749), v. 2, pp. 136–37; *Hymns* (1780), Hymn 212:1, 2, 4

4   *HSP* (1739), pp. 168–69; *Hymns* (1780), Hymn 26:4-6

5   *HSP* (1740), pp. 129–30; *Hymns* (1780), Hymn 218:1, 3-4

6   *Scripture Hymns*, v. 1, pp. 3–4; *Hymns* (1780), Hymn 117.1-2

7   *HSP* (1749), v. 2, pp. 313–14; *Hymns* (1780), Hymn 486.4-6

8   *HSP* (1740), pp. 1, 5–6; *Hymns* (1780), Hymn 4.1, 7–8

9   *Family Hymns*, pp. 54–55; *Hymns* (1780), Hymn 326.2-4

10   *HSP* (1740), pp. 224–25

11   *HSP* (1739), pp. 108–9; *Hymns* (1780), Hymn 186.2, 5

12   *CPH* (1738), pp. 51, 53; *Hymns* (1780), Hymn
        335:1, 4

13   *HSP* (1742), pp. 276–77; *Hymns* (1780), Hymn
        226.1, 3

14   *Scripture Hymns*, v. 2, p. 31

15   *Hymns for Children*, Hymn 15.1-2; *Hymns* (1780),
        Hymn 18.1-2

16   *HLS*, Hymn 155.5-6; *Hymns* (1780), Hymn
        418.5-6

17   *HLS*, Hymn 155.3-4; *Hymns* (1780), Hymn
        418.3-4

18   HLS, Hymn 153.2

19   *CPH* (1743), Psalm 150.1, 4

20   *HLS*, Hymn 157; *Hymns* (1780), Hymn 416

21   *HSP* (1749), v. 2, p. 246; *Hymns* (1780), Hymn
        465

22   *HSP* (1742), pp. 73–74; *Hymns* (1780), Hymn
        180.1, 4

23   *HSP* (1739), pp. 156–57; *Hymns* (1780), Hymn
        362.1-2

24   *HSP* (1749), v. 1, pp. 196, 212–13; *Hymns*
        (1780), Hymn 272.3, 2; Hymn 273.3

25   *HSP* (1749), v. 1, pp. 88–89; *Hymns* (1780),
        Hymn 383.1, 3, 8

26   *HSP* (1749), v. 2, pp. 321–22; *Hymns* (1780),
        Hymn 466.1-2

27   *HSP* (1740), pp. 182–83; *Hymns* (1780), Hymn
        506.3-4

28   *HSP* (1749), v. 2, pp. 320–21; *Hymns* (1780),
        Hymn 471.1-2, 5

29   *HSP* (1739), pp. 92–93; *Hymns* (1780), Hymn 128.1-2, 4-5

30   *HSP* (1740), pp. 62–63

31   *CPH* (1738), Psalm 139, part 1, vv.1, 4-5; part 2, v. 3

32   *Redemption Hymns*, Hymn 32.1-3, 5

33   *Redemption Hymns*, Hymn 50.1-2, 12, 24; *Hymns* (1780), Hymn 2.1-3, 9

34   *HSP* (1749), v. 1, pp. 38–39

35   *Scripture Hymns*, Hymn 1005; *Hymns* (1780), Hymn 293

36   *HSP* (1749), v. 2, pp. 230–31; *Hymns* (1780), Hymn 299.1, 4-5

37   *Scripture Hymns*, Gen. 17:1 and Gen. 1:26; *Hymns* (1780), Hymn 357.3-4

38   *HSP* (1742), pp. 30–31; *Hymns* (1780), Hymn 334.1, 4, 8

39   *HSP* (1739), pp. 206–8

40   *HLS*, Hymn 150

41   *Redemption Hymns*, pp. 11–12; *Hymns* (1780), Hymn 374.1, 3

42   *HSP* (1740), pp. 65–66; *Hymns* (1780), Hymn 130.1, 3, 6

43   *HSP* (1749), v. 1, pp. 236–38; *Hymns* (1780), Hymn 258.1, 4; Hymn 259.3

44   *Thanksgiving Hymns* (1759), Hymn 15.3-5

45   *HSP* (1749), v. 1, pp. 246–47; *Hymns* (1780), Hymn 315.1-3, 5

46   *Intercession Hymns* (1758), Hymn 2.1, 3-4; *Hymns* (1780), Hymn 430.1, 3-4

47   *HTTP*, Hymn 1.1, 4-5

48   *HSP* (1739), pp. 209–11

49   *Scripture Hymns*, v. 1, pp. 58–59; *Hymns* (1780), Hymn 309

50   *Scripture Hymns*, v. 2, pp. 170, 324; v. 1, p. 103; *Hymns* (1780), Hymn 396.1-3, 8

51   *HSP* (1740), p. 184; *Hymns* (1780), Hymn 507.3-4

52   *Redemption Hymns*, Hymn 34

INDEX TO THE FIRST LINES
OF THE HYMNS

HYMN TUNE AND METER INDEX

SCRIPTURE SOURCES CITED

ABOUT THE AUTHOR

PAUL WESLEY CHILCOTE is Professor of the Practice of Evangelism at Duke University Divinity School. He has been involved in theological education on three continents, serving as a missionary with his wife, Janet, in Kenya, and as a charter faculty member of Africa University in Zimbabwe. Dr. Chilcote served as Nippert Professor of Church History and Wesleyan Studies at Methodist Theological School in Ohio and helped launch the Florida campus of Asbury Theological Seminary.

Dr. Chilcote is author of twelve books, including *Praying in the Wesleyan Spirit; Her Own Story: Autobiographical Portraits of Early Methodist Women; The Wesleyan Tradition: A Paradigm for Renewal; Recapturing the Wesleys' Vision; Changed from Glory into Glory*; and *Early Methodist Spirituality.*

He serves as a unit editor in *The Works of John Wesley* project, is president of The Charles Wesley Society, and enjoys a special relationship with Mount Angel Abbey in Oregon as a Benedictine oblate. Dr. Chilcote is a frequent speaker and workshop leader in applied Wesleyan studies, particularly in the areas of spirituality, worship, discipleship, and evangelism.

OTHER BOOKS OF INTEREST

Changed from Glory into Glory:
Wesleyan Prayer for Transformation
Paul Wesley Chilcote
ISBN 978-0-8358-9814-0

Praying in the Wesleyan Spirit: 52 Prayers for Today
Paul Wesley Chilcote
ISBN 978-0-8358-0950-4

Forty Days to a Closer Walk with God:
The Practice of Centering Prayer
J. David Muyskens
ISBN 978-0-8358-9904-8

Creating a Life with God: The Call of Ancient Prayer Practices
Daniel Wolpert
ISBN 978-0-8358-9855-3

Leading a Life with God: Prayer Practices for Spiritual Leaders
Daniel Wolpert
ISBN 978-0-8358-1003-6

Talking in the Dark: Praying When Life Doesn't Make Sense
Steve Harper
ISBN 978-0-8358-9922-2

Find these books at your local bookstore
Call 1-800-972-0433 to order
Order online at www.UpperRoom.org/bookstore